DO NO[

This Is Only A Test

*To my na,
I hope that
that you enjoy
reading each page.
May you be enriched
by the principles that
we should live.

Sincerely
Ramona Roberson Gregory
2/1/2024!*

BY
Ramona Roberson Gregory

Table of Contents

Author's Biography

Ramona Roberson Gregory is affectionately known as Lisa to her family and friends. She is a native and current resident of Fort Lauderdale, Florida. She has served 8 years and 10 months in the United States Army after graduating from Dilliard High School in her hometown. Specialist Gregory served both in Europe and in the United States. Ramona is a mother of two adult children, Jasmine and Kevaris Gregory. She is an ordained minister, gospel recording artist, songwriter, play writer, comedian, and actress. Her musical accomplishments include a gospel music album, My Super Star, and 4 single records, along with being selected as a nominee for the South Florida Gospel Music Awards for Contemporary Artist of the Year. Her acting credits are Power Game 2 Believe (live stage play), Full Time Pimping (movie), and her own short skits.

Ms. Gregory's work careers include Cosmetology and Teaching. To her credit, she completed formal cosmetology education and was awarded a license as a cosmetologist and cosmetology teacher, performing hair services and instructing in several states. Ramona has previously co-owned her own salon, First Impressions Full-Service Beauty Salon. Ms. Gregory is currently employed as a Workshop Facilitator for a Career Center in Hollywood, Florida.

Simply known as Prophetess to her church family, Ramona earned a Bachelor's Degree in Biblical Counseling in 2010 from Master's International University of Divinity in Evansville, Indiana. Prophetess Gregory is currently the CEO of My Super Star Productions, His Chosen Vessels LLC, and Senior Ministry Leader of Acts Supernatural Assembly. Prophetess Gregory has served in several pastoral capacities for over 13 years. She currently serves the body of Christ as a prophet, teacher, and praise & worship leader.

Ramona enjoys going to the beach, movies, writing, scrapbooking, sewing, and of course, reading books. Her favorite sports include football, basketball, and wrestling.

--Ramona Roberson Gregory

Contact Information

Email: mysuperstarpro@gmail.com

Ministry Office 954-479-0315

Facebook: Ramona Roberson Gregory

Instagram: Ramona Roberson Gregory

Twitter: 1SuperStar

Dedication & Acknowledgements

All COVID-19 Survivors. Thanks be to God that you lived to tell your story.

Surviving family, friends, co-workers and neighbors who lost loved ones during the COVID-19 Pandemic. May your loved ones forever live in your hearts.

Essential Workers and First Responders (Medical Professionals, Medical Scientist, Law Enforcement, Educators, Clergy, Intercessors, etc.) Thanks for the countless sacrifices that you made to keep us safe and healthy, physically and mentally.

My mother Gwendolyn Copeland who always read books and always had books to read around the house, while I was growing up as a young girl at home. Therefore, I gained a great interest in reading books. I continued the tradition and I have even borrowed and returned books from your shelf in my adult years. The love of reading which led to loving books which led to me writing books. Mom, you are one of the few people that I know that joyfully accepts a book as a gift.

My lady author friends who inspired me to complete this project by going before me to publish their own book(s), Evang Brenda Williams "Beyond the Classroom." Evangelist Shakayl Cross "Poise Not Poison." Prophetess Gwendolyn M Rolle "Breaking the Silence." Lynn J. Brown "Things Mama Used to Say.", Pastor Chelec Pinckney "Back In Balance." Dr. Bishop Lois Delevoe "Reaching and

3

Awesome God Through Prayer." Some autographed your book for me, gave me a copy as a gift, or I purchased a copy, but either way, I am always proud to show off your book and say "My friend wrote this book" with a smile. Now I'm an official member of the "Christian ladies authors club." You all are phenomenal writers. I hope to follow your examples of being extraordinary in all that you do, because iron sharpens iron, and one man sharpens another.

My two lovely children Jasmine and Kevaris who are ways the first people to hear my ideas (like this book for instance) before the ideas come to fruition. Whatever I do, Kevaris always says "nice". Jasmine always says, "Good job mom." Thanks for believing that I can do all thing through Christ that strengthens me.

My family and friends who allowed me to record their stories of triumph over COVID-19 in this book. Your testimonies are sure to inspire people to trust in the power of God for healing of the mind and body. Thanks for allowing us to revisit with you behind the curtains to experience your feelings of fear, pain, uncertainty, and most of all the willingness to overcome all of adverse effects of COVID-19. Pastor Chelec Pinckney, Audie Silcott Sr., Brina Mills, Ruth Johnson, April Johnson, and Billy Mathis. Your accounts were chronicled as though we walked with you through it all.

The late Apostle David Q. Butler, my first father in the gospel. I know you would be so proud to hold this book in your hands of one of your many spiritual daughters and your favorite one (in my opinion) in the faith. Thanks for introducing me to salvation, signs, wonders and miracles.

My first major spiritual influencers were, Pastor Lue C. Bethea and Evangelist Sandra Dates Allen. You all invited me to church and to Christ and the rest is history.

My beloved parents, The late Charlie Roberson Sr. and the late Josephine Roberson. Gwendolyn Copeland and Reverend Milton Copeland. I treasure your examples of hard work.

A shout out to my siblings, just because, Christopher Thompson Sr., the late Charlie Ellis Roberson Jr, the late Charlie Ellis Roberson II, Indinia Dianna McKinney, Lynette Roberson Maxwell, Page Roberson Clark and Chastity Morris Williams. Keep being your amazing selves.

My beloved God-sister, the late Cheryl Denise Stroman. I sure could use your help on my up-coming book tours. I miss our girl time and travels.

Family, friends, co-workers, ministry co-laborers, brothers and sisters in Christ.

To the Amazon Publishing Library staff who brought this book to life. Thanks for your patience while you waited for me to start and finish the book. I am grateful for and your dedication in producing a product that "we" can be proud of.

Our Heavenly Father

As I have obeyed you, to deliver the revelations of this Coronavirus Pandemic to all who will receive, as you have delivered them to me.

Which He will manifest in His own time, He who is blessed and only Potentate, the King of kings and the Lord of lords. 1 Timothy 6:15

Do Not Panic; This Is Only a Test

Ramona Roberson Gregory

SYNOPSIS

"Do Not Panic; This Is Only a Test," is a reminder to us as we recall the valuable lessons learned from the Coronavirus Pandemic (officially announced in March 2020). Although now, years later, those who were affected by it, are still reaping the repercussions. This book combines both the actual and spiritual experiences that serve as a catalyst to make us wiser if ever faced with a similar crisis.

We acquired a wealth of applicable practical knowledge and understanding, by comparing natural healthy principles along with the supernatural healthy biblical principles. Whether personal, local, or worldwide, our lives can greatly benefit by humbly reflecting on this past dilemma. It is crucial that we show gratitude in our current post state and are empowered with strength and grace to endure future challenging situations like this one.

By enduring this catastrophic calamity, we have been equipped with the power to prevail over known and unexpected obstacles. Whenever we are faced with critical circumstances, we do not always know what we will do. But one thing we should not do is **"Do Not Panic."**

COVID-19 DISEASE

Coronavirus disease 2019 (COVID-19) is a contagious disease caused by the virus severe acute respiratory syndrome coronavirus 2SARS-CoV-2). The first known case was identified in Wuhan, China, in December 2019. The disease quickly spread worldwide, resulting in the COVID-19 pandemic. En.wickipedia.org.

Symptoms of COVID-19 are variable but often include fever, cough, headache, fatigue, breathing difficulties, loss of smell and loss of taste. Symptoms may begin one to fourteen days after exposure to the virus. At least a third of people who are infected do not develop noticeable symptoms. Of those who develop symptoms noticeable enough to be classified as patients, most (81%) develop mild to moderate symptoms (up to mild pneumonia), while 14% develop severe symptoms (dyspnea, hypoxia), or more than 50% lung involvement on imaging), and 5% develop critical symptoms (respiratory failure, shock, or multiorgan dysfunction). Older people are at a higher risk of developing severe symptoms. Some people continue to experience a range of effects long (COVID-19) for months after recovery, and damage to organs has been observed. Multi-year studies are underway to further investigate the long-term effects of the disease. En.wickipedia.org.

Transmission-COVID-19 The disease when infectious particles are breathed in or come into contact with the eyes, nose, or mouth. The risk is highest when people are in close proximity, but small airborne particles containing the virus can remain suspended in the air and travel over longer distances, particularly indoors. Transmission can also occur when people touch their eyes, nose, or mouth after touching surfaces or objects that have been contaminated by the virus. People remain contagious for up to 20 days and can spread the virus even if they do not develop symptoms. En.wickipedia.org.

Prologue

A federal public health emergency was declared and announced in the United States and other countries in the month of March in the year 2020. The world at large was introduced surprisingly and unwillingly to a pandemic by way of the Coronavirus, also known as COVID-19. Although the disease had become widespread at this time, it was already brewing and making a name for itself in Wuhan, China, reporting the first known case in December 2019. Therefore the 19 stands for the year 2019. This airborne disease was not contained where it began but traveled near and far.

My New Lifestyle During the COVID-19 Pandemic

A COVID Pandemic? How did we get here? Let me rewind. I remember some news reports one weekend in March 2020 about an airborne virus resembling the flu but much more aggressive. I wasn't overly concerned because I had faith that our healthcare system in America would come to the rescue of the citizens of the United States, and this threatening disease would be under control like a wayward child on a punishment.

The following week we discussed it at work with many wonders, few answers, and many more questions. Employed by a company that prided itself on great customer service, as a workshop facilitator, I was accustomed to cozy groups of eager learners in proximity.

Now I was instructed to make changes to that intimate interaction by separating customers by distancing them at every other desk, making wearing face masks now mandatory, and use of disinfectant measures more frequently. Cleaning and separating customers were understandable, but who teaches with their mouths covered up? This doesn't work well when your mouth is your "teaching tool" when your voice must be heard. Well, flexibility is always necessary in any job situation. As a matter of fact, that is one of my teaching lessons, so now it was time for me to practice what I taught. And in the grand scheme of things, I was proud to work for a company that cares enough about its employees to take necessary precautions.

I'll never forget the day that I went to the grocery store and pulled the door to enter. I observed a sign on the door that read, "No Face Covering, No Entry." Have I stepped into a science fiction movie or in a time chamber?

Wearing a mask or face covering in 2020 just to enter the grocery store? "I'll just go to another one," I reasoned. Well, as I drove around looking for a grocery store that was managed by sane management, I found out that this mandate spread faster than I could drive my car from one store to another. Who just has a face covering lying around just in case they need one in 2020? What a far-fetched, unheard-of idea. It is a good thing that I love scarves. I had plenty, enough to choose from and to share with a whole community of ladies if I needed to. Since I consider myself a fashionista, I chose one that would match my outfit, of course. As a cosmetologist, hair and make-up are my signatures. Grooming is my career. And I'm always dressed for success as an example to my customers, and that includes all public appearances, including grocery shopping.

It took me 20 minutes to apply my make-up just to cover up part of my face; so much for showing off my new blush and my new shiny lipstick. I was ready for this to be over already. However, I did find comfort in that my eyeshadow was popping. And at least I didn't have to cover my eyes.

After a full work week, I am active in my weekend gig job as a gospel recording artist. My calendar was booked with concert appearances that I was very much looking forward to. I received a call from a local well known music manager Jacqueline Hickman Singletary. It can be said of Mrs. Jackie like it is said of EF Hutton." When EF Hutton talks, people listen." "When Mrs. Jackie calls, people answer their phones." She called and granted me an opportunity to sing on stage at the Miami, Florida fairground for the first time. I was also booked by a church as 1 of the few Americans at a Caribbean Concert. Finally, a new audience that could appreciate Caribbean melodies. In addition to invites to my familiar hometown crowd. All were canceled without a rescheduled date.

While I pitied myself in my personal dilemma, transportation services had to create safe riding mandates, which created new regulations for airports, airlines, train stations, public buses, Uber, Door Dash, taxis, and roadside vehicle services. Safety precautions were put into place for educational facilities, retail stores, restaurants, doctor's offices, hospitals, public events, and even churches. Deaths and critical patients were now being reported on the news, report after report, channel after channel. Many hospital patients were isolated, unable to have visits from family and friends due to the rapid spread.

During one workday in March 2020, our company dismissed the employees to go work from home for two weeks while this virus cleared (we were told). Thereafter, our homes temporarily became our workspace. Our company's employees were equipped with telephones and computers to stay connected to our supervisors, customers, and each other. Prior to this, our customers, who we greeted warmly and shook hands with, became profiles online. As much as not having to travel to work daily was a reprise, I missed the daily interaction with my coworkers. We eventually returned to our company offices but with a strict policy of no visiting coworkers' offices. Everyone had to stay in their own office space. This seemed like punishment because our work staff really got along and truly liked each other. Visiting coworkers' offices, going to lunch together, celebrating birthdays, and having potlucks were activities that we looked forward to. Even our work center meetings took place on the Zoom platform, replacing us all being in the same room. But at least now we are within waving distance.

Wherever the Coronavirus was prevalent, companies were forced to find new creative ways to keep their workers safe, the doors to their businesses open, pay employees and continue to provide excellent customer service to their customers. Living rooms were turned into work offices, children's bedroom rooms were converted into classrooms, and hospitals, otherwise safe, became danger zones. Masks, gloves, disinfectants for surfaces and hands, and bathroom tissue were hoarded by panicking shoppers, with no concern about others in need of the same supplies. In-person interaction shifted to online virtual platforms and conference calls. Appointments had to be made for normal walk-in services. The virus that wreaked havoc on society and created chaos, which was expected to visit and dissipate within 2 weeks, was still an unwanted visitor 2 years later.

Unbelievable! This turn of events would make a best-selling book or box office movie. Unfortunately, it would be listed as a true story and not science fiction. While much of the world was confused and saddened by this recent turn of events, God-fearing people prayed, consulted one another, and picked up their Bibles for answers, comfort, and guidance. It was evident that the Centers for Disease Control (CDC), government officials, and medical personnel didn't have all the answers to all the questions being asked by desperate citizens scrapping to cope.

Everybody wanted to know. Can we, and will we survive? What shall we do in a time like this? Could it be that God is judging us? Is there a reference in the bible to this calamity? If so, what chapters and verses? Surely the prophets know what is happening.

According to Amos 3:7-8,*Surely the Lord God does nothing unless He reveals His secret to His servants, the prophets. A lion has roared. Who will not fear? The Lord God has spoken. Who can but prophesy?*

The Coronavirus Pandemic officially began, spreading rapidly, wreaking havoc, creating chaos, invoking fear, and leaving a trail of dead bodies behind.

Chapter 1: YOU ARE AN ESSENTIAL WORKER

And let us not grow weary while doing good, for in the due season, we shall reap if we do not lose heart. Therefore, as we have an opportunity, let us do good to all, especially to those who are of the household of faith. Galatians 6:9-10

Who Is Considered an Essential Worker and What Do They Do?

At the onset of the COVID-19 Pandemic, news reports emphasized the role of essential workers. While the job responsibilities highlighted were commonly known work fields, it was purposely noted that some jobs were prioritized as more essential than others.

First, we will start by defining essential and worker as defined by Oxford Languages Dictionary.

☐ *Essential-Absolutely necessary, important, crucial, key, vital, indispensable. **An employee, especially one who does manual or non-executive work that is informal; a person who works hard.***

☐ *Worker-A person who does a specified type of work or who works in a specified way. **A person who produces or achieves a specified thing: a toiler, workhorse, busy bee, an eager beaver, and a workaholic.***

As it currently stands, essential workers have been identified as ***doctors, nurses, and other front-line medical personnel. As well as janitors, maintenance professionals, grocery clerks, truck delivery drivers, postal workers, border patrol officers, transit employees, etc., who are classified as front-line workers, needed during difficult times.***

During times of crisis, whether it is personal, local, national, or worldwide, essential workers are of great necessity. In most of our lifetimes, we may have heard about or been affected by disastrous situations. Hurricanes, tornadoes, typhoons, tsunamis, floods, thunderstorms, lightning storms, volcano eruptions, sinkholes, and famines, which may have impacted your life in a minor or major way. Adding to the list are crimes of society like fraud schemes, political corruption, unfair treatment of the poor and disadvantaged, police brutality, civil unrest, burglary, robberies, killings, homicides, and suicides. The world is surrounded by horrific events daily, but we should never accept these events as being normal. As essential workers, we should find ways to make a positive impact in our communities by locating allocated resources to make a difference in difficult times. We are our brother's keeper.

Essential workers were, well, let's just say "essential" to this dreadful situation. They bore a large part of the responsibility to ensure that the deadly virus was contained and minimized. That also included careers that were not related to health care. There was, in essence, a state of "panic" in schools, public and private businesses, sports entities, and religious institutions. Many of these were temporarily closed by force, mostly due to local ordinances. The Centers for Disease Control (CDC), leaders of countries, states, providences, cities, and counties all scrambled to bring some understanding, order, and aid to calm the fears of its citizens while most of the world was in a panic.

From time to time in history, citizens near and abroad are touched directly or indirectly by unfortunate circumstances, including pandemics like the Coronavirus or COVID-19. Let's define medical terms that are related. We will use dictionary.com for the definition.

Pandemic-(adjective/noun)-(of a disease) prevalent throughout an entire country, continent, or the whole world.

*Epidemic-(adjective), also **epidemical** (of a disease), affects many persons at the same time and spreads from person to person in a locality where the disease is not permanently prevalent. Extremely prevalent & widespread. A temporary prevalence of a disease. A rapid spread or increase in the occurrence of something.*

Even though we face calamities in our lifetime, some are relatively new to the current generation. However, the Bible informs us disasters are not new to the world. Previously, there have been both weather and health catastrophic events. ***That which has been, is what will be, that which is done is what will be done, and there is***

nothing new under the sun. Is there anything that may be said, "See, this is new"? It has already been in ancient times before us. There is no remembrance of former things, nor will there be any remembrance of things that are to come by those who will come after.
Ecclesiastes 1:9-11

The 10 Plagues of Egypt

The Bible gives us many case scenarios concerning times of crisis. One of which happened early in civilization. Bible history records the 10 Plagues of Egypt, which are found in Exodus Chapters 7-12. The account is a story about a supreme God versus a supreme ruler known as a Pharoah or King and a prophet and intercessor by the name of Moses.

Pharaoh is the vernacular term often used for the monarchs of ancient Egypt, who ruled from the First Dynasty (c. 3150 BC) until the annexation of Egypt by the Roman Empire in 30 B.C. However, regardless of gender, "king" was the term used most frequently by the ancient Egyptians for their monarchs through the middle of the Eighteenth Dynasty during the New Kingdom.

Pharaoh held absolute power in Egypt. Besides being the supreme commander of both the army, and navy he was chief justice of the royal court and a high priest of the country's religion. Pharaoh was considered a god by his people, the reincarnation of the Egyptian god Horus.

Pharaoh's likes and dislikes were sacred rulings, the same as the laws of the Egyptian gods.

This arrogant mindset guaranteed a clash between Pharaoh and Moses. Exodus says God "hardened Pharaoh's heart," but Pharaoh first hardened his own heart by refusing to let the enslaved Israelites go. After all, they were free labor, and they were "Asiatics" considered inferior by the racist Egyptians. <u>Wikipedia</u>

This resembles the same stunt that the United States and other countries pulled by classifying certain people groups and exploiting their gifts and talent. Though many have lost their lives in the struggle for freedom and acceptance, I am grateful for all the liberties that minorities enjoy today.

When Pharaoh refused to repent after the 10 plagues, God set him up for judgment that would result in Israel's freedom. Finally, after Pharoah's army was swallowed up in the Red Sea, he realized that his own claim to being a god and the power of the Egyptian gods was simply make-believe. <u>Learningreligions.com</u>

The 10 plagues occurred due to the Pharoah's disobedience to God. The water turned to blood, infestations of frogs, lice, flies, livestock pestilence, boils, and locusts. Hail, total darkness, and the killing of firstborn children of both people and animals. One of these alone is horrible, but 10, one after the other, is incomprehensible. Imagine the daily breaking news that would have made the headlines if the current news media outlets, video cameras, electronic tablets, and camera phones were readily available to report these unusual happenings in that ancient time.

Picture going to the beach for rest and relaxation, only to arrive and discover that the beautiful blue-green water is now a bloody red ocean. Or, if taking your boat out for deep sea fishing, there were no ocean creatures alive to catch. All have died a bloody death and are stinking, rotting, and floating. On a hot day when you are parched, your choice of drink is a bloody cup of water to quench your thirst. Dying of dehydration may have been an honorable way to be remembered. The river and all water sources of oceans, lakes, ponds, and home fountains were all full of blood. Exodus 7:14-25

Frogs and flies everywhere you sit, step, and lay. In your bed, croaking on the couch, hoping in the shower, crawling on kitchen cabinets, and overtaking the refrigerator, flying on your food, and swimming in the pool. Forget about a night's rest with bedfellows and the disturbing loud buzzing noise of these pesky creatures who have invaded your inside dwelling and outdoor space. Exodus 8:1-15 and 8:20-32

A pestilence on livestock. Camels, sheep, horses, assess, and oxen were diseased by pestilence making common animal meat unable to be consumed. Making the modern-day "mad cow disease" seems like a minor inconvenience.

Pestilence-(noun) a contagious or infectious epidemic disease that spreads quickly and is often fatal, like the Bubonic plague. Merriam-webster.com

Mad Cow Disease-Formally known as Bovine Spongiform Encephalopathy (BSE), "Mad Cow Disease" is a persistent food safety concern in the U.S. and abroad. BSE occurs when cattle are fed rendered meat products made from other dead, disabled, or diseased cattle or sheep as a feed supplement or when chickens are fed rendered animals, and their manure is mixed into cattle feed.

Tissue from infected cows' central nervous systems (including the brain or spinal cord) is the most infectious part of a cow. Such tissue may be found in hot dogs, taco fillings, bologna, and other products containing gelatin, as well as a variety of ground or chopped meats. People who eat meat from infected animals can contract the human version of the disease, known as variant Creutzfeldt-Jakob Disease (vCJD). The disease slowly eats holes in the brain over a matter of years, turning it sponge-like, and invariably results in dementia and death. There is no known cure, treatment, or vaccine for vCJD. https://www.centerforfoodsafety.org

This case scenario of pestilence would make converting over to becoming a vegan or vegetarian an easy decision, except the locusts ate up all the fruits, vegetables, and plants in Exodus 9:1-7. One square mile of a locust swarm contains more than 100,000,000 insects, and modern swarms have covered as much as 400 square miles. Where were the Egyptian gods Isis and Seth that they depended on to protect their harvest? Perhaps asleep like Elijah concluded on Mt. Carmel in 1 King 18:27-29. It looks like their God was taking a nap during this whole ordeal.

It is expected that the sun will set after a day full of sunlight, and we will curtail our daytime activities accordingly. For instance, after an evening of work, watching a movie in the dark makes the story more dramatic and scarier if it is classified as horror or suspense. However, thick darkness all day, during the morning hours, at noon, afternoon, and evening is unfathomable. Perhaps this is where the term "I can't see my hand in front of my face" was derived from. This weather occurrence defied the sun gods Re, Amun, Aten, and Horus. The account of the darkness is told in Exodus 10:21-29. The Egyptians served gods that could not say, "Let there be light," and light appeared, like our God, the creator of the universe, can and did.

Then God said, "Let there be light,"; and there was light. And God saw the light, that it was good; and God divided the light from the darkness. God called the light day and the darkness He called Night. So, the evening and the morning were the first days. Genesis 1:3-5

Being plummeted by hail is not considered playing in the snow or having fun snowball fights. Constant hail on humans and animals causes bodily harm and extensive injury to property as it did to the Egyptians. Insurance

23

companies now have special policies for "hail damage" because it is so destructive and cost insurance company's large payouts. This was an incredible event because the rain was not consistent in Egypt. It was rare for it to rain. It did not only rain but also froze to make the hail and join forces with other elements. Combining a mixture of hail, thunder, and fire. What a dangerous, unusual weather pattern that the meteorologist didn't predict. Hiding under the bed or in the closet until it was over may have seemed reasonable until it may have been realized that the roof and window damage to their homes didn't provide any shelter. In addition, there was the possibility of the fire burning the house down. And who could stop the deafening noise of hail, thunder, fire, and piercing screams? Only the God who started it all when He was good and ready. Again, the Egyptians had to wait out yet another plague miserably.

Now if you picture small annoying pellet size hail or medium size golf ball size hail pellets, let me bring you up to date on the incredible size and damage that hail does in our modern-day weather catastrophes. Here are some recent headlines.

GRAPEFUIT-SIZE HAIL SLAMS NORTH TEXAS IN "LOADED GUN ATMOSPHERE (weather.com, by Johathan Belles, May 23, 2020). Quote from the article, "This kind of hail is dangerous and can be deadly for anyone outside while stones of this size are falling."

50,000 GOLF BALLS HIT AT ONCE. MASSIVE HAIL RAINS DOWN IN HOWELL(Michigan). (Fox2Detroit-News, June 16,

2023, by Hilary Golston). "Basically, a nasty hailstorm came through about 4:45 yesterday. The storm came out of nowhere (and) within 15 minutes, 3 inches of hail was on the ground. Every crop I have on this farm," said CJ Turner, owner of Bentley Lake Farms. Mother Nature can be nasty at times, and the hail received on Thursday was magnificent to behold and devastating in effect, Turner, who said he had 85 acres of crops destroyed. "Sweet potato, melon, tomatoes, onions, green beans, everything you can think of," Turner said. "It's a big hit in my back pocket. I'll have to recover. It's too late to plant; other things I can replant." In total, he says he lost $500,000 worth of crops.

*HAIL ANNIHILATES FRUIT AND VEGETABLE CROPS AT A FARM NEAR HOWELL AS FURTHER BEGINS TO START OVER (*WXYZ Detroit, by Kimberly Craig, Howell, Mich, June 16, 2023). "It came down so hard that it sounded like I was standing under a freight train. It was unbelievable," said farmer C.J. Turner of Bentley Lake Farms in Marion Township near Howell.

Baseballs are big, and melons are huge in hail size. In my imagination, it is possible that the Lord bumped the size up so that there would be no mistaking that He was at work, to basketball size (that's not in the Bible, only in my mind) was a great possibility. It was large enough to destroy all their crops, injure people, property, and animals, causing animals to have to be sheltered and people to retreat to hide.

Thunderstorm- a violent short-lived weather disturbance that is almost always associated with lightning, thunder, dense clouds, heavy rain or hail, and strong gusty winds. Britanica.com

There are different kinds of thunderstorms, some more severe than others, spinning off from different weather patterns, moving at different speeds, causing various damage, and threatening lives and property.

Thunderstorms are identified as *Single-cell, Multi-cell, Squall line, Super Cell, Bow Line, Mesoscale Convective System (MCS), Mesoscale Convective Complex (MCC), Mesoscale Convective Vortex (MCV), and Derecho thunderstorms. Get details of these phenomenal storms.* *https://www.nssl.noaa.gov*

As a child growing up in Florida (where lightning and thunderstorms are fearful and deadly), we were told a myth; that when it was thundering and lightning, the Devil was beating his wife. (That's how I found out that the Devil was married). She must a been a bad wife, the way the lightning and thunderstorms roared (Maybe they got a divorce because I see that she is not mentioned in the scriptures. LOL).

Fire-combustion or burning, in which substances combine chemically with oxygen from the air and typically give out bright light, heat, and smoke. Oxford Languages. We don't need a fancy definition of fire. We know all we need to know. It's destructive and deadly. Adding fire to the hail and thunderstorms only resulted in gloom and doom.

Three Health-Related Plagues in Egypt

The Lice, Boils, and firstborn deaths were direct attacks on the body. Lice infestation was recorded in Exodus 8:16-19. Although I have never suffered from lice, as a licensed cosmetologist, I am familiar with lice infestation. If a lice-infected person comes into a salon, the whole salon (whether there is small or large amounts of customers) must be dismissed immediately. Lice jump from one place to another and one person to another. If people aren't evacuated quickly, they may go home with some unwanted pesky guests. The salon then must be disinfected per licensing ordinances. The home and car of the person must have the same regime. And the only sure cure for the person affected is to shave all their hair off all over the body. I emphasize all hair all over.

Some of us who went through the Coronavirus Pandemic wondered if this virus was created in a laboratory and released on mankind by some mad scientists. This theory has not been proved, and no verdict has been handed down to support or negate this common thought. However, in the case of the lice infestation in Egypt, the jury concluded that Prophet Moses was directly responsible, of course, under the instructions of God.

So, the LORD said to Moses, "Say to Aaron, 'Stretch out your rod, and strike the dust of the land, so that it may become lice throughout all the land of Egypt." And they did so. For Aaron stretched out his hand with his rod and struck the dust of the earth, and it became lice on man and beast. Exodus 8:16-17

Boils were another health-related plague. *Boils are inflamed and painful abscesses breaking into a running (fluid leaking) sore.* That is the tasteful definition. A boil is an outward growth with crusted skin, oozing with blood and pus (You may not want to eat and read this chapter simultaneously; you've been warned).

In Exodus 9:8-11, obviously the Egyptians had boils because it manifested on their bodies. Boils could show up anywhere, everywhere, on anybody. Normal movements like walking, sitting, laying down, or scratching were now nearly impossible without excruciating pain, leaving a trail of dead skin, blood, and pus. This is the disease that the patriarch Job, one of the wealthiest men in the Bible, suffered from in Job 2:7-10. His wealth didn't prevent him from this damnable disease. One true statement that we can say about the Coronavirus is that it did not discriminate. Rich, middle class, and poor all were affected alike.

One of the well-known facts about the Coronavirus is that a person may be asymptomatic and may not be aware that they have been affected, which can cause unknown spreading of the disease. In the case of the boils, everyone had it, and everybody knew it.

Asymptomatic-a person affected by a condition but producing or showing no symptoms of it. Oxford Languages

The Coronavirus symptoms, according to combined information from cdc.gov and search.yahoo.com, include but are not limited *to shortness of breath or difficulty breathing, muscle aches, chills, sore throat, runny nose, headache, chest pain, pink eye (conjunctivitis), nausea, vomiting, diarrhea, rash, cough, fatigue, new loss of taste or smell and chest congestion.*

These are also symptoms of other illnesses like colds and affluenza (flu). For one to have a proper diagnosis, a conclusive test must be rendered by trained medical personnel. There are reports that some initial COVID-19 tests came back with incorrect results, so the people who were ill had to be retested. How a person feels in their body is a large consideration and must be parallel with the medical report. But there doesn't seem to be any indication of doubts that the Egyptians were covered with boils. No second opinion was needed.

There is nothing in any of these accounts of the plague that are pleasant. But sadly enough, the Egyptians, their servants and their animals all lost their *first-born* children. I'd rank this as the worst of the plagues. Whom you are connected to also does affect your life for better or worse. The servants and animals were innocent bystanders who suffered due to the stubbornness of Pharoah. As you follow the story, it is repeated that they were victims in many of these instances. Fathers, mothers, siblings, grandparents, aunts, and uncles are all in simultaneous mourning, along with the animals lowing in the fields. What gut-wrenching sights and sounds. Dead people, both male and female, babies, teenagers, young, middle-aged, and elderly. Corpses inside houses, outside houses, in the fields, in the streets, in water sources, on rooftops, and on horseback. There was no discrimination on gender or age. As a parent, I could imagine that the parents shook their children and shouted, "Wake up, wake up, please wake up," hoping that this awful occurrence somehow missed their family. One thing I am sure of is God never misses. What God does; He does on purpose. All He simply asked was for Pharoah to let His people go. These are the results of saying no the God.

The cries and shrieks must have been heard miles away. This whole situation was wreaked with loss and death. This may be one of the times we may consider applying, "I wouldn't wish this on my enemy." If only the King had allowed the Israelites to worship on God's terms and timing, these accounts would have ended on a positive note.

Does this remind us of our plight during the COVID-19 Pandemic? The caskets and graves were short, medium, and long. The disease didn't have mercy on anyone, anywhere.

Unfortunately, the Egyptians were not only enemies of the Israelites but enemies of God. **For we know Him who said, "Vengeance is Mine, I will repay," says the Lord. And again, "The Lord will judge His people." It is a fearful thing to fall into the hands of the living God.** Hebrews 10:30-31

After the Egyptian firstborn was killed, that was the turning point of Pharoah from temporary insanity to temporary sanity. He came to his senses after a short time. He then again became permanently insane and reneged on letting the children of Israel go. Therefore, God drowned him and his army in the Red Sea as they pursued the Israelites for the last time.

The question can be posed, "What calamities can be avoided if nations would allow those who want to worship God the liberty to do so, without laws to the contrary?

According to the Matthew Henry Bible Commentary, let us look at the significance of these plagues.

☐ The Nile River, which became blood, was considered sacred water.

☐ The Egyptians honored the frog God Hapi and Goddess Heqt.

☐ The cattle represented the sacred bull Apis, God Ptah & Goddess Hathor.

☐ The gods of the harvest were Isis and Seth.

☐ The sun gods were Re, Amun, Aten, and Horus.

Modern Day Idols

Therefore, we can conclude that the God of all gods showed up and displayed His power and majesty. Citizens of the United States and other countries serve other gods besides the True and Living God. We may not bow down and worship them in a physical way, but we "serve" them with our time and money. Now, we will revisit how idol worship was halted during the height of the Coronavirus Pandemic.

☐ *Sports* athletes are sacred celebrities. Sports games were canceled.

☐ *Entertainers* are revered and idolized. A wide variety of shows were canceled.

☐ *Properties* are prized status symbols. Commercial and personal property became overpriced and vacated.

☐ *Material possessions* are personal accumulations of pride and wealth. Sick people couldn't enjoy what they had labored for. Their material things couldn't bring them comfort.

☐ *Religious activities* consist of worshipping religions & denominations more than worshipping God. Churches were mainly on online platforms. Some churches closed and never reopened.

☐ *Medical professionals* by which we have replaced the healing power of God with modern medicine. Pills have taken the place of prayer. Their medical intelligence couldn't discover a cure for the Coronavirus.

☐ *Finances* determine the classification of the poor, middle class, and rich or wealthy. Poor people could only afford to pray. Middle-class folks ran out of employee health benefits. Some rich and wealthy spent money on premium health care and still died.

There were endless reports of COVID-19 deaths. As of 6/3/2023, it was reported a total of 6,885,926 died worldwide. Not just of the firstborn, but of all ages, races, and nationalities. Loss and death were also the themes of the Coronavirus. We had daily reminders of employment cuts, repossessed properties, overcrowded hospitals with insufficient equipment, and funeral waiting lists to bury loved ones.

Food Shortages

During the pandemic ordering food and supplies was more than a convenient option. It was a wise safety measure. If you were brave enough to go to the grocery store, it was reported that shelves were unusually bare of usually plentiful items. Food shortages were common during the pandemic, but there were bona-fide famines in Biblical days. It was more dismal than shoppers not being able to find their favorite ice cream.

Famine-an extreme scarcity of food. A great shortage. A ravenous appetite

Merriam-webster.com

Now we shall recall one of the famines during the life of Prophet Elijah in 1 Kings 17:1. ***Now Elijah the Tishbite, from Tishbe in Gilead, said to Ahab, "As the Lord, the God of Israel, lives, whom I serve, there will be neither dew nor rain in the next few years except at my word. "*** Prophet Elijah not only announced that there was going to be a famine, but he had to live and endure the drastic situation himself. God sent ravens to feed him; thereafter, the brook Cherith that he drank from dried up, causing Prophet Elijah to become a house guest of a widow woman for food to survive. The power of prayer worked a miracle, so they did not run out of food during the famine according to 1 Kings chapter 17. There were miracles happening during the COVID-19 devastation. We just could not depend on the new outlets to make it breaking news.

Some people prayed more intensely during the Coronavirus pandemic and increased their faith, while others decreased or stopped praying due to disappointment in their conditions.

As voices on the earth, we declare, "These are the last days," "These are perilous times," "The world is soon coming to an end," "Jesus is soon to come," but our recognition of the time we are living in doesn't exempt us from the impact of the situations we live in. Remember, Noah prophesied the world-wide flood but had to build an ark for himself and his family to escape drowning. Genesis chapters 6-9

During the height of the Coronavirus spread starting in 2020, we experienced shortages of food and other products due to transportation and production difficulties in the United States and abroad. But those temporary inconveniences don't compare to the devastation of biblical proportions during the time of Prophet Elisha, Prophet Elijah's understudy. Like prophet-like protegee.

People were more than desperate in 2 Kings 6:24-25. *At this time, there was a great famine in Samaria; and indeed, they besieged it until a donkey's head was sold for eighty shekels of silver and one-fourth of a kab of dove droppings for five shekels of silver.* Warning, this story is not for the squeamish or faint of heart.

King Ben-Hadad of Aram sieged Samaria to capture the tribe of Israel. According to yahoo.com, *a siege is a military operation in which enemy forces surround a town or building, cutting off essential supplies, with the aim of compelling the surrender of those inside.*

The citizens could not go outside of the city for daily needs, nor would the enemy army allow allies to bring in necessary needs either. This caused whatever was being sold to drastically increase in price because both the buyers and sellers were desperate for survival. Donkeys were unclean animals, according to the Mosaic law, an unacceptable sacrifice. Nor was this animal found on the gourmet menu in the local restaurants. Normally, God's people didn't eat any parts of donkeys. But now, donkey heads are a source of survival for any hungry person.

Shekel *came into the English language via the Hebrew Bible, where it is first used in the Book of Genesis. The term* *"shekel" has been used for a unit of weight, around 9.6 or 9.8 grams (0.34 or 0.35 oz), used in Bronze Age Europe for balance weights and fragments of bronze that may have served as money.* Google.com shares this fact.

Of course, our money measurements are different, but we can conclude that there was price gouging going on at extreme levels. Bird waste was now useful, used for cooking (like coal) if you even had something to cook during the famine.

Cab/kab was about 1-quart in U.S. comparison.

The fact that someone had to scrap up bird droppings and sell them as a business to feed themselves and their families is enough to tell us how appalling the situation was. Desperate times cause desperate measures. Literal ·measures of 1 quart.

Those in the Coronavirus Pandemic were inconvenienced by limited mobility, therefore, people favored ordering food and supplies over frequenting crowds of shoppers to guard their health. But our moments of being uncomfortable pale in comparison to these biblical accounts.

Isn't this all too familiar? We watched fuel, food, water, rent, property, and more increase to unimaginable and unreasonable amounts, due to trade inconveniences, cargo problems, shortage of food, materials, and goods. Some retailers were forced to raise prices, and consumers were forced to pay the prices. However, some companies just took advantage of desperate citizens who were grappling to survive.

My sign that "Jesus may be soon to return" was when I went to the $1 Dollar Tree store, and the prices read everything $1.25. A sudden increase of one whole quarter. Not a gradual increase of 5 to 10 cents. We needed our extra quarters to use for the rising fuel, rent, mortgage, insurance, and food prices. I was convinced the world was coming to an end very soon. But I'm glad I was wrong. The prices didn't go back to $1.00, I still shop there, and the world has not ended. Prophets miss it sometimes.

God's Kingdom Essential Workers

Now I'd like to call to your attention a time when essential workers were needed for God's Kingdom purposes. Towards the end of the life of Jesus Christ, He was betrayed by one of his own disciples of his inner circle, Judas Iscariot in St. John 13:21-30. Jesus Christ was arrested, falsely accused, whipped, beaten, humiliated, scorned, and ultimately killed, as is recorded in St. John chapters 18-19.

Jesus Christ lost his life to unjust brutality like so many men with dark skin tones. His death reminds us of the reason we had recent protests like Black Lives Matter (BLM) to commemorate the hostile, untimely death of

George Floyd during the pandemic by members of the police force that was called to investigate an incident involving George.

On May 25, 2020, George Floyd, a 46-year-old black man, was murdered in Minneapolis, Minnesota, U.S., while being arrested on suspicion of using a counterfeit bill in a neighborhood store. During the arrest, Derek Chauvin, a white police officer with the Minneapolis Police Department, knelt on Floyd's neck for nine minutes and 29 seconds after he was handcuffed and lying face down. wikipedia.org

Angry people, including me, took to the streets all over the world (I marched in Miami, Florida) with masks on and marched for justice. George couldn't speak; as a matter of fact, some of his last words were, "I Can't Breathe." and "Mama." So those of us who cared and were afraid to send our sons to the corner store, spoke for him, and justice was served in a court of law, although it would not bring him back to life, his family stood in his stead. George Floyd himself never got his day in court, unlike Jesus, who did. However, the Lord was still crucified without a cause, even after the judge heard His side.

Our Lord and Savior was tried by governing officials and in the court of public opinion. Prior to His arrest before His crucifixion, Jesus never had a criminal record containing a misdemeanor or felony, but he was nevertheless charged with crimes. His charges were exhaustive: preaching the gospel, teaching the word of God, restoring hope to the hopeless, testifying about his Father God, healing the sick, raising the dead, performing miracles, casting out demons, challenging the scribes and Pharisees, restoring families, and increasing faith of the doubters.

Jesus Christ's death placed his disciples and followers in a crisis. They were disgusted, disoriented, distraught, discouraged, and discombobulated. The savior, friend, prophet, and teacher whom they had grown to know, and love was falsely accused and died a humiliating death. The only hope they had was His promise to rise from the grave, and He did. So once again, they hailed their beloved savior, but unfortunately for them, it was only temporary. He rose just long enough to give them a message and to ascend to heaven until the appointed time of his return. St. John chapters 20-21

Essential Workers Charge

According to St. Matthew 28:16-20, the eleven disciples (Judas committed suicide) went away into Galilee, into a mountain where Jesus had appointed them. And his final directive and message to them were, in essence, "You Are Essential Workers." Jesus Christ gave his disciples and apostles a charge. Though the situation surrounding His death didn't call for a worldwide medical plan a like the Coronavirus Pandemic did. First, there wasn't the same type of media coverage. Now we have the benefit of cable, internet, satellite, cellular phones, tablets, laptops, and desktop computers. Both good and bad news travels at the same speed.

But the word had to be spread throughout the earth, not just the city or state, that Jesus was the Savior of the World. He was crucified and had risen again. Now these essential workers had a charge to spread the good news.

To understand the importance of the last words of Jesus to the disciples, let us fast forward and compare it to a ceremony of sorts in modern-day settings. To ensure that essential workers understand the charge, political officers, military personnel, medical doctors, and witnesses in a courtroom take oaths to verbalize their duties and responsibilities in front of senior officers and other witnesses. They are sworn to the words they speak as the truth of their intentions. Most officials must swear by the Bible.

Oath- A solemn, usually formal calling upon God or a god to witness to the truth of what one says or to witness that one sincerely intends to do what one says.

A solemn attestation of the truth or inviolability of one's words.Merriam-webster.com

Oath of Office-We will use a simplified explanation that enlightens the importance of oath ceremonies from bensguide.gpo.gov. In the Federal Government, for an official to take office, he or she must first take the oath of office; this is also known as a swearing-in ceremony .

The official reciting the oath swears an allegiance to uphold the Constitution. The Constitution only specifies an oath of office for the President; however, Article VI of the Constitution states that other officials, including members of Congress, "shall be bound by Oath or Affirmation to support this Constitution."

Executive Branch: President and Vice President of the United States-In order to assume his or her duties, the President-elect must recite the Oath of Office. The oath is administered by the Chief Justice of the Supreme Court. The President-elect places the left hand on the Bible, raises the right hand, and takes the oath as directed by the Chief Justice. The oath, as stated in Article II, Section I, Clause 8 of the U.S. Constitution, is as follows:

"I do solemnly swear (or affirm) that I will faithfully execute the office of President of the United States and will to the best of my ability, preserve, protect and defend the Constitution of the United States."

The Vice President also takes an oath of office. Until 1933, the Vice President took the oath of office in the Senate; today, both the President and Vice President are inaugurated in the same ceremony.

"I do solemnly swear that I will support and defend the Constitution of the United States against all enemies, foreign and domestic, that I will bear true faith and allegiance to the same: that I take this obligation freely, without any mental reservation or purpose of evasion,

and I will well and faithfully discharge the duties of the office on which I am about to enter. So, help me, God."

Officials must take these oaths to serve in the highest government office in the United States. I have taken this oath above to serve in the United States Army. Surely, God has us take godly oaths to serve in the highest government in the world, the Kingdom of God. In essence, the whole Bible, all of God's commands is the oath. bensguide.gpo.gov.

The Great Commission Oath

Perhaps, Jesus had them raise their right hands and place a hand over their heart to repeat after Him when He said: *"Go ye therefore, and teach all nations, baptizing them in the name of the Father, and of the Son, and of the Holy Ghost: Teaching them to observe all things whatsoever I have commanded you: and, lo, I am with you always, even unto the end of the world. Amen.*

St. Matthew 28:18-20

When we are born again, we all take that oath consciously, unconsciously, and by default. It's what we signed up for. I have always been amazed as a 9-year veteran of the United States Army when soldiers try to avoid wartimes. One of the sole reasons for enlisting is to serve and protect our country. Some are more interested in traveling to see the world, college funds, and career training. Those are nice perks that make the commitment attractive, but we enlist to serve and protect our county, as the oath that we had to repeat out loud says.

Some followers of Christ seem to be oblivious as to why they are needed as helpers, prayer warriors, witnesses, or in other words, "essential workers." They are more interested in blessings, healing, wealth, and prosperity. When we lose sight of our responsibility as essential workers, helping others is no longer a priority, then helping others becomes a byproduct.

Just as there are essential workers for worldly affairs, there are essential workers in God's Kingdom to present salvation for healthiness and wholeness. Which of these responsibilities did you fulfill as an essential worker during the Coronavirus pandemic?

☐ Prayer for the sick, recovering & front-line medical personnel?

☐ Comforted grieving families who lost their loved ones?

☐ Spoken words of encouragement to the discouraged?

☐ Checked on neighbors, family, friends, and especially the elderly?

☐ Provided your resources to those who had insufficient?

☐ Passed out food at local food banks to those who were in need?

☐ Provided someone a ride that was without transportation?

☐ Cooked meals for someone without food or electricity?

☐ Covered a co-worker's shift while they cared for a sick family member?

☐ Gave or lent money to someone who lost their job?

Just because the COVID-19 Pandemic is no longer a worldwide threat does not relieve you of your duties as a caring citizen and essential worker in your community and in the Kingdom of God. Whatever you did to help is admirable, and remember, God sees all your works and kindness. But your work is not done.

Due to the severity of the state-of-affairs, many front-line essential professionals quit their jobs, causing shortages in pertinent roles. Don't you quit! Your community needs you, and the Kingdom of God needs you too.

Then He said to them, ***"The harvest truly is great, but the laborers are few; therefore, pray to the Lord of the harvest to send out laborers into His harvest.*** *St. Luke 10:2*

YOU ARE AN ESSENTIAL WORKER!

Chapter 2: FIRST RESPONDERS, LET'S GO!

After these things, the Lord appointed seventy others also, and sent them two by two before His face into every city and place where He Himself was about to go. Then He said to them, "The harvest truly is great, but the laborers are few; therefore, pray to the Lord of the harvest to send out laborers into His harvest.

St. Luke 10:1-2

Who Are First Responders and What Do They Do?

First Responders have been instrumental during the COVID19 Pandemic to help their communities to be informed, safe, and healthy. Who is considered a First Responder according to the Center for Disease Control (CDC)?

A first responder is a person with specialized training who is among the first to arrive and to provide assistance at the scene of an emergency, such as an accident, natural disaster, or terrorism. First responders typically include law enforcement officers, including state troopers, deputies, all federal law enforcement-based agents, security officers, and school resource officers. As well as paramedics, emergency medical technicians, firefighters, rescuers, military personnel, sanitation workers, public

works, and other trained members of organizations connected with this type of work. In some areas, emergency department personnel are also required to respond to disasters and critical situations, designating them first responders.

In other words, first responders are the first called and the first to give assistance in a time of crisis. They are trained and specialize in offering aid in the most difficult situations. Let us examine the facts from the National Institute of Health (NIH).

First responders, including police officers, firefighters, and emergency medical services (EMS) personnel, are essential workers required to interact with the public, and in the midst of the Coronavirus disease 2019 (COVID-19) pandemic, their work has become particularly visible. Often at the forefront of the pandemic, these first responders have a high risk of exposure to COVID-19-positive individuals in the course of their job duties. Due to this increased risk of exposure, research has shown that first responders have a three-fold higher rate of COVID-19 infection compared to members of the general population. Due to this increased risk of exposure, research has shown that first responders have a three-fold higher rate of COVID-19 infection compared to members of the general population.

COVID-19 Working Conditions

Beyond their work-related exposure risk, the first-responder workforce has also faced other challenges due to the COVID-19 pandemic. Personal protective equipment shortages, particularly at the beginning of the pandemic, prevented some first responders from having the appropriate equipment to protect themselves from infection. In addition, with the high incidence of COVID-19 infection in first responders, there was the challenge of workforce depletion. Furthermore, the protests sparked by the deaths of Breonna Taylor, George Floyd, and others, which occurred predominantly in May and June of 2020 during the COVID-19 pandemic, also strained first responders as increased work hours were required and safety concerns around both violence and COVID-19 exposure were heightened.

Beyond the effects and consequences of COVID-19 infection, first responders have also experienced increased stress and anxiety, and research suggests that over half of frontline providers and first responders are concerned about their mental health in the context of the COVID-19 pandemic. Specifically, first responders and frontline providers have reported increased feelings of sadness and anxiety, with a reluctance to ask for help. First responders may also experience effects from being stigmatized due to their high exposure to COVID-19, leading to feelings of isolation. Finally, social distancing, both on the job and in personal households, may affect first responders' abilities to seek and receive support from their networks of coworkers, friends, or family. Ultimately, the challenges faced by first responders during the COVID-19 pandemic may be contributing to a decreased likelihood that they remain in their occupation (NIH).

There was a tragedy that went down in world history worse than the Coronavirus Pandemic. This incident needed first responders and essential workers to respond. This happened a long time ago, before COVID-19. Maybe you have heard about it. During the life of Jesus Christ when he lived in the earth, He, His disciples, and is followers were in a crisis. Jesus had been arrested and crucified. He died a horrible and inhumane death. Jesus Christ, the Son of God, hope for all mankind, and the much-anticipated Messiah, made headline news.

I could imagine that CNN, ABC, or NBC would have aired the story with pictures, commentary, details, and witnesses. The death of Jesus was the saddest story ever told, but His resurrection was the greatest story ever told. The Lord Jesus was humiliated, killed and buried in the tomb. And upon rising again, the first responders came to His aid. All four of the gospel writers recorded this historical biblical event. Let us review the account in the book of St. Mark chapters 15 and 16.

First Responders of Christ's Crucifixion

Simon of Cyrene *responded* by bearing the cross of Jesus. These 2 different translations indicate that Simon did not volunteer, but he bore the responsibility and took the opportunity to help Jesus in His time of need, even though he didn't want to in St. Mark 15:21. Simon took upon himself a burden that was too much for Jesus to bear at that time. He had been scrouged (beaten) before the crucifixion. Jesus Christ was very weak and suffering severe pain, and this was just the beginning of His humiliation.

As the soldiers led him away, they seized Simon from Cyrene, who was on his way in from the country, and put the cross on him and made him carry it behind Jesus. NIV New International Version.

As the crowd led Jesus away to his death, Simon of Cyrene, who was just coming into Jerusalem from the country, was forced to follow, carrying Jesus' cross. NLT New Living Translation.

The chances that there is one person who *wants* to put their own lives in danger to save the lives of others is probably slim to 0. But there are job responsibilities that demand this level of commitment. The oath. Firefighters, Police officers, EMTs, doctors, and nurses do *want* to help people. But they don't *want* to necessarily put their own health at risk to save others. However, they do every day. They didn't *want* to be isolated from their family or work short-staffed. Being a first responder is about putting the needs of others as a high priority, even if it means inconveniencing yourself. These professions are literally hands-on jobs; there is no other way. As much as the Lord loves us, even He tried to bargain with God for another way to redeem man.

And He was withdrawn from them about a stone's throw, and He knelt down and prayed, saying, "Father, if it is Your will, take this cup away from Me; nevertheless, not My will, but Yours, be done." St. Luke 22:41 **There was no other way to redeem man.**

During the crisis that Jesus Christ suffered, some first responders stepped up for duty.

A Roman Soldier *responded* by giving Jesus a drink as He was dying. As He hung on the cross, He said, **"I thirst."** St. John 19:28-30. What kindness to give the Lord His last drink. Perhaps that is why it was said that a blessing follows those who give a righteous man a drink of water. Now there are two trains of thought that are debated by scholars as to the motive of offering Jesus a drink.

☐ Giving Jesus a drink was mocking or making fun of Him, knowing he was going to die anyway. The drink was not a cold sweet cup of Kool-Aid, but sour wine that was normally prepared for soldiers and a drink prepared for the poor. This mocking would have been an extension of how He was treated when arrested.

Then they spat in His face and beat Him, and others struck Him with the palms of their hands, saying,

"Prophesy to us, Christ, Who is the one who struck You?
St. Matthew 26:67

Then the soldiers of the governor took Jesus into the Praetorium (official residence of a Roman governor) and gathered the whole garrison around Him. And they stripped Him and put a scarlet robe on Him. When they had twisted a crown of thorns, they put it on His head and a reed in His right hand. And they bowed the knee before Him and mocked Him, saying, "Hail, King of the Jews!" Then they spat on Him and took the reed and struck Him on the head. And when they had mocked Him, they took the robe off Him, put His own clothes on Him, and led Him away to be crucified.
St. Matthew 27:27-31

We would say today that they added insult to injury. A second scholarly belief highlights an opposite perspective.

☐ Giving Jesus a drink may have been showing compassion by helping to ease some of the pain. Either way, he refused the drink in St. Matthew 27:33-34. Even if He would have drunk it, death was still the ultimate end. There may have been some soldiers that believed He was the Messiah but had to carry out their duties anyway lest they be killed. Often, we hear people in their profession remove their feelings from a situation and say, "I'm just doing my job."

Offering sour wine combined with gall (a bitter poisonous herb/plant) to our suffering, crucified Lord Jesus may have been a medicinal and merciful gesture to dull the intense pain, but St. Luke in his holy gospel implies that the drink offered to our Lord Jesus at His crucifixion was part of the torture. "*The soldiers also mocked Him, coming and offering Him sour wine*" St. Luke 23:36. suscopts.org.

It is believed that this herb/plant is akin to the poopy plant, which is used to make opium, a pain killer used by modern doctors prescribed to patients in pain. However, this is also misused as an unprescribed street drug. Therefore, it is plausible to believe that it had pain-killing properties. However, the motive is what is in question. Was this bitter drink given to him by the soldier to mock Him? Or for compassion to help him bear the pain? Let's use the compassion theory for this instance.

Countless medical professionals probably went home in tears every day because their efforts failed to keep someone alive who died of COVID-19. Resuscitation, respirators, medications, operations, monitors, and rehabilitation efforts all failed. Doctors had to go into the waiting room time after time to share the grim news of another loved one gone too soon. Young, middle-aged, and elderly. As with Jesus, temporary relief was offered, but death was imminent, just as the doctors and nurses could only offer a few comforts while they inevitably waited for the sick patients who lost the battle with the Coronavirus to succumb after all their medical efforts were exhausted. Jesus Christ also knew when He approached the last seconds of His life.

After this, Jesus, knowing that all things were now accomplished, that the Scripture might be fulfilled,

said, "I thirst!" Now a vessel full of sour wine was sitting there, and they filled a sponge with sour wine, put it on hyssop, and put it to His mouth. So when Jesus had received the sour wine, He said, "It is finished!" And bowing His head, He gave up His spirit. St. John 19:28-30

Joseph of Arimathea *responded* by caring for the battered and tormented body of the Lord Jesus. He went to Pilate and voluntarily asked for Jesus' body so that He could have a dignified, honorable burial fit for a King. Joseph was a rich wealthy Jewish man who is believed to be an uncle of Jesus. Joseph disagreed with the crucifixion plot of the government. Joseph offered a much-needed service to an innocent man. Jesus the crucified Lord was wrapped in fine linen and placed in a new tomb. St. John even detailed that Joseph had the body of Jesus removed from the cross. St. John 19:38-42

His kindness is so significant that it is recorded in all 4 gospels. Joseph of Arimathea is venerated as a saint by the Catholic and Eastern Orthodox Churches and in some Protestant traditions. It was so important, that the Holy Spirit had the writers to record this act of compassion. He was a member of the Sanhedrin Council, which was the highest court system, mirroring our highest court in the United States, the Supreme Court.

The Sanhedrin was an assembly of either 23 or 71 elders (known as "rabbis" after the destruction of the Second Temple) appointed to sit as a tribunal in every city in the ancient Land of Israel. There were two classes of

Rabbinite Jewish courts which were called Sanhedrin, the Great Sanhedrin, and the Lesser Sanhedrin. *Wikipedia*

I have heard and seen many times that rich people or people of celebrity status pay for the final burial of strangers whose lives and deaths have impacted society in some way. Normally the wealthy lead in financial campaigns, giving large sums of money and offering their resources in natural disasters, unfortunate occurrences like COVID-19 and for murder victims killed.

Floyd Mayweather takes care of George Floyd's funeral.

Floyd "Money" Mayweather is a professional top-ranked boxer for the World Boxing Association. He is also a boxing promoter.

Although he "did not want to talk about" it publicly, boxing legend Floyd Mayweather paid the funeral expenses for George Floyd in June 2020. Floyd's death at the hands of Minneapolis police in May was the impetus for ongoing nationwide protests against police brutality.

Shaq pays for Florida athlete's services (Dexter Rentz).

(Shaquille O'Neal is a retired professional National Basketball Association star).

In late April 2020, a drive-by shooting in Orlando, Florida fatally injured 18-year-old standout athlete Dexter Rentz. After hearing about Rentz, who had signed to play football with the Louisville Cardinals, Orlando resident

Shaquille O'Neal stepped in. "This one hurts my heart," **O'Neal told ESPN**. "I wish things like this would never go on. It's just so sad, and I want to be able to help his family. I wanted to take care of it." O'Neal told Rentz's parents he'd pay for "whatever his mom wants," including a horse and carriage and custom-made casket.

NBA player *Harrison Barnes* and NFL player *Malik Jackson* pay for police-shooting victim's funeral. These 2 pro-athletes and one of their wives paid for Atatiana Jefferson's funeral.

After three seasons with the Dallas Mavericks, NBA star Harrison Barnes says he felt like part of the Texas community. That's one reason he was so affected by the tragic shooting of Atatiana Jefferson in her Fort Worth home in October 2019. Jefferson, 28, was playing video games with her nephew when a police officer responded to an "open structure call" at her home. The officer shot Jefferson through a closed window. "It was a tragic situation that happened," Barnes told NBC Sports. The 27-year-old athlete and his wife Brittany paid for 90% of Jefferson's funeral expenses. His friend, Philadelphia Eagles defender Malik Jackson, paid the remainder.

These are just a few examples of the kindness of the wealthy just as Joseph of Arimathea show to Jesus Christ.

Many businesses slowed down or closed, during this pandemic, but funeral homes business increased in volume and revenue. Funeral professionals are ministers. They serve the family by properly preparing loved ones for burials. Joseph was purposeful in giving the Lord an honorable funeral. St. Matthew 27:57-61

Nicodemus *responded* by helping Joseph of Arimathea (above) with the body of Jesus by wrapping Him up and preparing His body with herbs. It appears that Nicodemus maybe even helped to remove Him from the cross or was at least present. This account is found in St. John 19:38-42. Prior to this tragedy, Nicodemus came to Jesus by night to ask Him questions. In one conversation, Jesus explained to him what it meant to be born again. Nicodemus must have felt honored to have had personal time with the Lord to have his questions answered and receive new revelations. Nicodemus most likely felt like it was an honor to handle the body of the Lord, who had enlightened him more than any of his diligent studies had revealed. John was purposeful in including the part that Nicodemus contributed by using the words "also and "they."

After this, Joseph of Arimathea, being a disciple of Jesus, but secretly, for fear of the Jews, asked Pilate that he might take away the body of Jesus; and Pilate gave him permission. So, he came and took the body of Jesus. And Nicodemus, who at first came to Jesus by night, also came, bringing a mixture of myrrh and aloes, about a hundred pounds. Then they took the body of Jesus and bound it in strips of linen with the spices, as the custom of the Jews is to bury. Now in the place where He was crucified, there was a garden, and in the garden, a new tomb in which no one had yet been laid. So, there

they laid Jesus because of the Jews' Preparation Day, for the tomb was nearby.

A big thanks is deserved to everyone who helped anyone through the COVID-19 Pandemic with medical care, a meal, or a word of hope.

His Mother & Other Women *responded* by attending the crucifixion and, most of all, going to the tomb the morning of the resurrection to check on the Lord Jesus. They were faithful followers from the cross to the tomb.

Near the cross of Jesus stood his mother, his mother's sister, Mary the wife of Clopas, and Mary Magdalene. St John 19:25

Now on the first day of the week, very early in the morning, they, and certain other women with them, came to the tomb bringing the spices which they had prepared. It was Mary Magdalene, Joanna, Mary, the mother of James, and the other women with them, who told these things to the apostles. St. Luke 24:1-10

There were also women looking on from afar, among whom were Mary Magdalene, Mary the mother of James and of Joses, and Salome, who also followed Him and ministered to Him when He was in Galilee, and many other women who came up with Him to Jerusalem. St. Mark 15:40-41

Jesus had a group of women disciples who helped with the ministry work and provided personal financial assistance and resources. St. Luke 8:3

Mary the mother of Jesus, Mary the mother of James and Joses, Mary the wife of Clopas, Joanna wife of Chuza (Jesus' aunt & uncle), Salome mother of James and John, were specifically named. However, there were many other women who were not named, but surely their names are written in the Lambs Book of Life. If you are a first responder in your home, family, neighborhood, and community, you too will be rewarded. Making it through the Coronavirus Pandemic is a reward.

May God abundantly bless all the countless nurses, doctors, surgeons, scientists, EMTs, Law Enforcement personnel, Chaplains, and Ministers, the first responders that served on the front lines.

Angels *responded* by rolling the stone away, giving the women a message and commanding them to alert the disciples of Jesus Christ rising in St. Mark 16:5-6. God sent angels to comfort those who arrived at the tomb and to serve as a witness to the great resurrection of Christ.

And entering the tomb, they saw a young man clothed in a long white robe sitting on the right side; and they were alarmed. But he said to them, "Do not be alarmed. You seek Jesus of Nazareth, who was crucified. He is risen! He is not here. See the place where they laid Him. But go, tell His disciples and Pete that He is going before you into Galilee; there you will see Him, as

He said to you." So, they went out quickly and fled from the tomb, for they trembled and were amazed. And they said nothing to anyone, for they were afraid.

But Mary stood outside by the tomb weeping, and as she wept, she stooped down and looked into the tomb. And she saw two angels in white sitting, one at the head and the other at the feet, where the body of Jesus had lain. Then they said to her, "Woman, why are you weeping?" She said to them, "Because they have taken away my Lord, and I do not know where they have laid Him." St John 20:11-14

God *responded* by "receiving Jesus into heaven to sit next to Him on the throne."

According to St. Mark 16:19, *So then, after the Lord had spoken to them, He was received up into heaven, and sat down at the right hand of God.* Now that Jesus had fulfilled the His role as the lamb that was slain before the foundation of the world, His words that He spoke on the cross, "It is finished," were complete. Therefore, God welcomed Jesus, His only begotten Son, to take His seat beside Him once again.

God, the Very First Responder

Of course, this wasn't the first tragedy that God had to respond to, and it won't be the last. Let us go back to the beginning of mankind before Jesus Christ walked the earth.

The first humans needed God to save them. The difference was that their situation was self-inflicted.

Adam and Eve were the first humans in an emergency situation, who needed a first responder. After being removed from the garden because of their disobedience in blatantly eating from the Tree of Good and Evil, Father God came to their rescue.

As soon as they disobeyed, God was on the scene and made clothes out of animal skins for Adam and his wife to wear in Genesis 3:21. When we call for help to first responders, we need and expect expedient service, quick, fast, and in a hurry. If you call 911, the dispatchers will send the emergency workers who will get there as fast as is humanly possible. They may come faster than you expect, slower that you expect, when you expect or not at all (cases have been reported) but know this, God is omnipresent. Before you call, He is already there. Jesus was already slain for our sins before the foundation of the world as it states in Revelation 13:8.

God is our refuge and strength, very present help in trouble. Psalms 46:1

"It shall come to pass that before they call, I will answer, And while they are still speaking, I will hear. Isaiah 65:24 **God is a first responder!**

FIRST RESPONDERS, LET'S GO!

Chapter 3: COVID-19 CHRIST OVER VIRUSES, INFECTIOUS DISEASES

Is anyone among you suffering? Let him pray. Is anyone cheerful? Let him sing psalms. Is anyone among you sick? Let him call for the elders of the church, and let them pray over him, anointing him with oil in the name of the Lord. And the prayer of faith will save the sick, and the Lord will raise him up. And if he has committed sins, he will be forgiven. Confess your trespasses to one another, and pray for one another, that you may be healed. The effective, fervent prayer of a righteous man avails much.
James 5:13-16

COVID-19 Acronym

During the height of the Coronavirus Pandemic, there was a definition circulating on social media, created to give meaning to the acronym of COVID-19. Christ Over Viruses, Infectious Diseases 19. I can't claim to be the one who made this up, however that was genius. Never-the-less, I was willing to share it and speak it, because this describes the power of our Lord. This meaning gave hope to so many people who were suffering, letting them know there is a power greater than what the medical professionals could offer. An ultimate divine power. After all, we must keep in mind that they are physicians "practicing" medicine.

A round of applause and a standing ovation is due to our medical professionals, wherever the Coronavirus affected their communities. Placing their own health at risk to help others daily is admirable. This is a solemn oath that they took to be able to wear the title doctors and nurse etc.

Working extended hours, few meals, away from family with bare minimal comforts between shifts and patients. It takes a special grace to dispense such care. Much of our hope was in the health care system and the medical specialist during this treacherous time. Whether they were in the hospital receiving patients, EMTs responding to emergencies outside of the hospital, pharmacy professionals dispensing medications, maintenance teams cleaning, disinfecting and sterilizing, or scientists in the labs attempting to create a cure, they all are deserving of much appreciation.

Although there were so many lives lost so quickly, there were many lives that were saved. The medical staff had the unfortunate task of pronouncing death and delivering the grim news to many heart-broken families. They also had the joy of saving lives and giving good news to some hopeful families.

The news reports during the height of the Coronavirus Pandemic included the "numbers" of how many people died or were infected with COVID-19. According to the worldmeters.info (update June 13, 2023). These are recent numbers.

Coronavirus Cases:

690,303,517

Coronavirus Deaths:

6,890,725

Coronavirus Patients Recovered:

662,764,190

The weather, stock market, international affairs, wars, political topics and even crime were not so important anymore. Hospital staff were now the "stars" of the news broadcast with their gripping stories of all the people dying from the Coronavirus or barely holding on to their last breath. Death makes the news, increase views and ratings. Lives saved don't have the same sensationalism. Or the media doesn't always share news objectively and allow the audience the opportunity to see the full picture.

Although the Coronavirus claimed a magnanimous number of lives, it has been reported that people survived this dreaded disease but not reported publicly often by news stations. The stories of survival were told from person to person and from one social media platform to another. Coronavirus survivors were delighted to share the good news and most attributed their ability to survive to God. For the span of about 2 years there was a news report on television or social media on some aspect of COVID-19 spreading. Depressing and devastating.

Recovery information could be found if researched, but it wasn't plentiful in the news.

Some lost their lives due to the Coronavirus while some lives were spared. Why did some people die, and others did not? Why was there divine intervention for some and not others? There is not one blanket answer. Even Godly, Spirit filled believers met their demise. That is one of those questions we may have to ask God in heaven, if we even care to know or think on these horrific earth experiences. It probably won't be a thought in our mind once we taste the glory of heaven.

A lingering question for many was, where did this execrable disease come from? Was it manufactured in a laboratory by enemies, scientist, or friend-enemies?' Is it a judgement from God? Is it a curse from Satan? We may not all agree on the origin, but it is safe to say that we do agree that COVID 19 is detestable, awful, and deadly.

The question was not, Why people were or are getting sick? But instead, Why was or are so many people are sick at one time? There seemed to be more questions than answers. Disease affects every one's body differently. Doctors and health experts make determinations as to how mild or severe a medical condition is by several factors. Any single disease may fall within several classifications The most widely used classifications of disease are the following Britannica.com

(1) **Topographic**-by bodily region or system.

(2) **Anatomic**-by organ or tissue.

(3) **Physiological**-by function or effect.

(4) **Pathological**-by the nature of the disease process.

(5) **Etiologic**-(causal) causing or contributing to the development of a disease or condition.

(6) **Juristic**-by speed of advent of death.

(7) **Epidemiological**-the branch of medicine that deals with the study of the causes, distribution, and control of disease in populations.

(8) **Statistical**-contributing factors that influence disease.

A widely known fact reported in the reputable news outlets was that medical professionals, other first responders, and essential workers, quit their jobs due to the mandatory vaccination regulations for staff, and in part due to exhaustion. Longer shifts, understaffed, sometimes working without the proper personal protection equipment or inefficient medical machines and medications to help the patients. And sheer fear of being possibly infected from having to be in proximity. First responders like medical personnel must touch to heal.

Healing Prayers at a Distance

Speaking of touching to heal, in most religious gatherings people who believe in the power of prayer are accustomed to touching people to pray healing for them. It is common to see ministers place anointing oil on the person receiving prayer and place their hands on the area of concern or just on the sick person's forehead. During the Coronavirus pandemic praying for people in person became a "touchy" situation (pun intended). Rules were set during this time in hospitals and health facilities which prevented ministers, family members and visitors from being present to lay hands on their parishioners, family, and friends. This directive almost seemed like a violation of the right to pray in person for the sick. Clergy and laity alike had to pray from afar and trust that distance was not a barrier for God to move by their heart of the compassion. Where we can't physically go, God is already there. He spoke these words concerning the children of Israel and they are applicable to us today.

Then they cry unto the LORD in their trouble, and he saveth them out of their distresses. He sent his word and healed them and delivered them from their destruction. Oh, that men would praise the LORD for his goodness, and for his wonderful works to the children of men! Psalm 107:19-21.

The hand of the person praying is usually placed on the body during prayer to locate the diseased body part as a point of contact. There is something comforting about a personal touch. It shows care and compassion at its highest level. But during the Coronavirus Pandemic faith had to be stretched to reach near and far across the miles to other cities, states, and countries. So then, faith caused many who suffered to be healed without being touched. We find several "touchless" healing stories in the scriptures. Let us review one.

There is a story of a gentleman from Capernaum in the Bible, a centurion (roman military commander), who relieved Jesus Christ from going to his house (quite the opposite of many seeking Jesus) and preferred that the Lord spoke at a distance to heal his servant. Jesus volunteered to go the centurions house, but was told by the centurion homeowner who was seeking prayer, that would not be necessary. He didn't believe his house was worthy of a King to enter. Turn down Jesus making a personal visit to your home for any reason is unheard of to say the least. Christ made many house calls, so the state of the house clean or unkempt wasn't the issue to Him. The issue was the centurion's heart. He didn't feel worthy. Maybe his house was clean, but his heart was dirty. Or perhaps he was just completely humbled the Jesus Christ would even accept an invitation to come to his home. As for me, I reasoned that the centurion's decision was rude and insensitive. As we say in our modern-day vernacular "Where do they do that at?"

As busy as Jesus was with his ministry and proteges, it was an honor for Him to schedule this in his time in his travels. However, Jesus was not offended, as a matter of fact, Jesus was impressed and called his actions exercising faith. As an affirmation, Jesus granted him his request and the centurion's servant was healed. St. Matthew 8:5-13

Now when Jesus had entered Capernaum, a centurion came to Him, pleading with Him, saying, "Lord, my servant is lying at home paralyzed, dreadfully tormented." And Jesus said to him, "I will come and heal him." The centurion answered and said, "Lord, I am not worthy that You should come under my roof. But only speak a word, and my servant will be healed. For I also am a man under authority, having soldiers under me. And I say to this one, 'Go,' and he goes; and to another, 'Come,' and he comes; and to my servant, 'Do this,' and he does it." When Jesus heard it, He marveled, and said to those who followed, "Assuredly, I say to you, I have not found such great faith, not even in Israel! And I say to you that many will come from east and west, and sit down with Abraham, Isaac, and Jacob in the kingdom of heaven. But the sons of the kingdom will be cast out into outer darkness. There will be weeping and gnashing of teeth." Then Jesus said to the centurion, "Go your way; and as you have believed, so let it be done for you." And his servant was healed that same hour.

Who Was Praying for People Who Didn't Have the Coronavirus?

While prayer was going up all over the world for the COVID-19 patients to be healed, and for God to work miracles and raise the dead. The Lord gave me a startling revelation. I took to social media to share this warning.

68

Surprisingly the Holy Spirit shared with me that while the world was praying to eradicate COVID-19, we were leaving many other sick and afflicted people uncovered from prayer, because we became single focused on the Coronavirus, as though this was the only disease in the world. I believe this to be a trick of the enemy to get us looking in one direction while He moved in another.

The Spirit of the Lord posed this question to me. If most everyone is praying for COVID-19 patients, who is praying for the other people suffering from different sickness, disease, natural disasters, and tragedies? "Good question God", which is why He is God. He sees the things that are out of our focus. People around us were dying from car accidents, cancer, drowning, fires, mass shootings and committing suicide, but we forgot to add them to our prayer list. Since it was not my sole responsibility to pray for the sick. I engaged my social media family to pray for those suffering from ALL manners of disease. We spent hours in sessions solely praying.

Medical professionals categorize illness as acute and chronic etc. to distinguish the severity of a disease. Some sicknesses are considered worse than others, depending on how it affects the body. There are many components to sickness and disease individually, or communicably. Family genetics, health, lifestyle, diet, desire to live, health care, environment, support, and faith are a few of the contributing factors.

No matter the disease the power of the Holy Spirt can heal ALL. One thing that I do know is that God through the

69

Holy Spirit is not experiencing a "shortage" of healings and miracles for any kind of diseases. Both the Old Testament, New Testament, and modern-day church beyond the book of Acts have left on record the proof of Gods power to make our minds and bodies healthy and whole (COVID19 survivor stories are shared in the book). There are miracles of all kinds in the scriptures. Let us look at the ones specifically that dealt with health issues. Here are a selected few.

Miracles and Healings in the Bible

☐ King Jeroboam's hand instantly withered and then was restored by a man of God (1 Kings 131-6).

☐ The Widow of Zarephath's son became sick and died, but afterwards was raised from the dead by Prophet Elijah (1 Kings 17:7-24).

☐ The Syrian army was smitten with blindness by Prophet Elisha at Dothan and then their sight was restored (2 Kings 6:15-20).

☐ King Hezekiah was healed of a boil after God sent the Prophet Isaiah to tell him to get his house in order and prepare to die. (2 Kings 20:1-11).

☐ The woman with the spirit of infirmity who was bowed (bent) over and in no wise could lift herself up was cured (Luke 13:10-17).

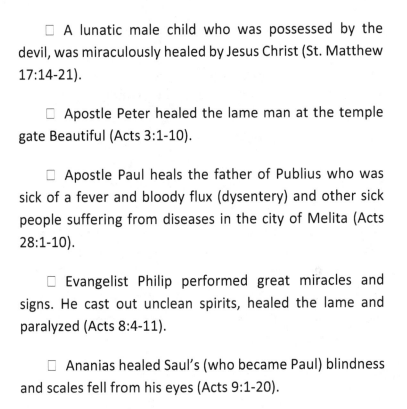

☐ A lunatic male child who was possessed by the devil, was miraculously healed by Jesus Christ (St. Matthew 17:14-21).

☐ Apostle Peter healed the lame man at the temple gate Beautiful (Acts 3:1-10).

☐ Apostle Paul heals the father of Publius who was sick of a fever and bloody flux (dysentery) and other sick people suffering from diseases in the city of Melita (Acts 28:1-10).

☐ Evangelist Philip performed great miracles and signs. He cast out unclean spirits, healed the lame and paralyzed (Acts 8:4-11).

☐ Ananias healed Saul's (who became Paul) blindness and scales fell from his eyes (Acts 9:1-20).

It's impossible to have every statistic of every person who ever took ill during the COVID-19 Pandemic. Just as we don't have every miracle or occurrence of healing in the Bible. Not everything that Jesus, His prophets, or His disciples did by way of signs, wonders and miracles are recorded. But we have enough to know that God's dispensed His power to heal the sick and afflicted as He still does now.

When reading the Bible, we have an innate mindset that these tantalizing stories of the lame walking, the blind seeing, and the dead being raised only happened in Biblical

71

times. Aren't we still living in Biblical times? Isn't the Bible still relevant today? Isn't it recorded in St. Matthew 24:3 that "Heaven and earth shall all pass away, but my word will last forever?" It is thoroughly understood that modern day examples help to increase our faith and brings us real life experiences and we can serve as witnesses to the great power of God. Research the lives of great men and women of God, mostly known as Evangelists like: Smith Wigglesworth, Aimee Semple-Mc-Pherson, Oral Roberts, R.W. Shambach, Kathryn Kuhlman, John G. Lake, William J Seymour, Derek Prince, Dr/Bishop Gertrude Stacks and Mildred Hicks just to name a few. You will find that that same illness that were healed in the Bible, were healed by these chosen vessels of God. You are also chosen to carry on the same works just like these generals of the faith did, post the book of Revelation.

And there are also many other things that Jesus did, which if they were written one by one, I suppose that even the world itself could not contain the books. John 21:25 NKJV

The people saw the apostles perform many miracles and do amazing things. The believers had a common faith in Jesus as they met on Solomon's Porch. Acts5:12 NKJV

Any sickness you name does not present a problem to God. Through the power of the Holy Spirit, He can work miracles instantly and bring gradual healing too. Either way the result will be health and wholeness.

72

The Coronavirus or any disease didn't or don't scare God, though it scares us. God didn't have go into the Board Room of Heaven and meet with the heavenly host to come up with a plan as to how to eradicate this disease from plaguing most of the globe. He was already ahead of us. For those of us who serve God and trust in the sacrifice of the Lord Jesus Christ, once we become born again; miracles, healings, blessings, and provision come as a package deal. Claim your total package. Live in health and wholeness.

You don't have to wait for some major health problem to come your way to apply these healing promises. Speak healing over your headache, broken arm, or a toothache. Meditate on one of the most powerful life changing scripture passages that follows concerning total body healing in Isaiah Chapter 53.

1. Who has believed our report? And to whom has the arm of the Lord been revealed?

2. For He shall grow up before Him as a tender plant, And as a root out of dry ground. He has no form or comeliness; And when we see Him, there is no beauty that we should desire Him.

3. He is despised and rejected by men, A Man of sorrows and acquainted with grief. And we hid, as it were, our faces from Him; He was despised, and we did not esteem Him.

4. Surely, He has borne our griefs and carried our sorrows; Yet we esteemed Him stricken, Smitten by God, and afflicted.

5. But He was wounded for our transgressions, He was bruised for our iniquities; The chastisement for our peace was upon Him, And by His stripes we are healed.

6. All we like sheep have gone astray; We have turned, every one, to his own way; And the Lord has laid on Him the iniquity of us all.

7. He was oppressed and He was afflicted, Yet He opened not His mouth; He was led as a lamb to the slaughter, And as a sheep before its shearers is silent, So He opened not His mouth.

8. He was taken from prison and from judgment, And who will declare His generation? For He was cut off from the land of the living; For the transgressions of My people He was stricken.

9. And they made His grave with the wicked-- But with the rich at His death, Because He had done no violence, Nor was any deceit in His mouth.

10. Yet it pleased the Lord to bruise Him; He has put Him to grief. When You make His soul an offering for sin, He shall see His seed, He shall prolong His days, And the pleasure of the Lord shall prosper in His hand.

11. He shall see the labor of His soul, and be satisfied. By His knowledge My righteous Servant shall justify many, For He shall bear their iniquities.

12. Therefore, I will divide Him a portion with the great, And He shall divide the spoil with the strong, Because He poured out His soul unto death, And He was numbered with the transgressors, And He bore the sin of many, And made intercession for the transgressors.

Surely you have prayed for yourself and someone else or many other people, and the Holy Spirit moved on your behalf and performed miracles and healing. Your name may not be in the Bible, you may never have been interviewed by a major magazine, you may not be recognized among the popular preachers, but your prayers count too. Not matter what sickness or disease you are faced with in your life or the life of others, pray, "do not panic", and always remember:

CHRIST OVER VIRUSES' INFECTIOUS DISEASE!

Chapter 4: SOCIAL DISTANCING, STAY 6 FEET AWAY FROM SIN

Be not deceived: evil communications corrupt good manners. Awake to righteousness, and Sin not; for some have not the knowledge of God: I speak this to your shame.1 Corinthians 15:33-34

During the Coronavirus pandemic, everyone had 2 choices. One was to separate 6 feet on top of the ground, or two was to be separated 6 feet under the ground. I chose the former. In other words, social distance voluntarily or be permanently social distanced. Door number 1 or Door number 2? Social distance became a popular term during the time of COVID-19. So even though dictionaries are already crowded with words, and lots of them, words had to scoot over and make room for one more new word "social distance."

The Collins English Dictionary, Merriam-Webster Dictionary, and the Oxford English Dictionary, the three main English-language dictionaries, added social distancing to their lists last year (2020), a product of the coronavirus pandemic that swept the globe in 2020. news.harvard.edu

What Is Social & Physical Distancing?

Social distancing, also called "physical distancing," means keeping a safe space between yourself and other people who are not from your household. To practice social or physical distancing, stay at least 6 feet (about 2 arms' length) from other people who are not from your household in both indoor and outdoor spaces.

Social distancing is the practice of increasing the space between individuals and decreasing the frequency of contact to reduce the risk of spreading disease (ideally maintaining at least 6 feet between all individuals, even those who are asymptomatic). Social distancing strategies can be applied on an individual level (e.g., avoiding physical contact), a group level (e.g., canceling group activities where individuals will be in close contact), and an operational level (e.g., rearranging chairs in the dining hall to increase the distance between them). cdc.gov. The common mandate was:

☐ Social and Physical Distancing-6 feet apart

☐ Isolation-14 days alone

Purpose of Social & Physical Distancing

..... practiced in combination with other everyday preventive actions *to reduce the spread of COVID-19.* stacks.cdc.gov

Social Distancing Plus Other Safety Measures

This safety method was one of the answers to *slow the spread* of the disease, by keeping people farther away from each other, which reduces the risk of transmitting the disease from one person to another. As helpful as social distancing is; it is not an answer alone. The CDC emphasized that all safety measures must be combined to keep oneself as safe as possible. Any and everything that kept us safe we employed.

Social distancing should be practiced in combination with other everyday preventive actions to reduce the spread of COVID-19, including wearing cloth face coverings, avoiding touching your face with unwashed hands, and frequently washing your hands with soap and water for at least 20 seconds. stacks.cdc.gov

Isolation Due to COVID-19

In addition to social distancing in public or with family, isolation was suggested to keep the maximum distance away from others even in the home.

If you had a positive COVID-19 test, please self-isolate at home as much as possible according to CDC instructions. If there are other people in your household who do not have COVID-19, please try to separate yourself from them in a different room or area of your

household, and wear a face covering if you must be around other people (see CDC isolation instructions).

Some patients with severely weakened immune systems or who were severely ill from COVID-19 (for example, required oxygen support or intensive care in the hospital) may need a longer 20 day isolation period; see the CDC website for details and consult your health care provider if you have questions. rush.edu

Social Closeness

Hugs, kisses, laughs, giggles, staring into another's eyes, cuddling, sitting or lying on another's lap, tickling, and sharing food are common outward showings of affection. Handshakes and pats on the back are a sign of respect and pleasant greetings. These are normal human interactions woven into the fabric of many cultures. However, the Coronavirus brought all these lovey-dovey public and private displays to a screeching halt.

Here is a snapshot of expressions of affection before the COVID-19 Pandemic:

☐ Hugs were plentiful in the house of worship. Parishioners greeted each other with warm hugs and "holy" kisses on the cheek.

☐ Husbands and wives shared a passionate kiss before leaving for their jobs and again upon returning home.

☐ Parents kissed their kids on the forehead or cheek as they dropped them off at school or the bus stop and again upon returning home.

☐ Families snuggled closely together on the couch covered with blankets for movie night.

☐ Job interviewers and job candidates gave firm handshakes to each other.

☐ Friends and family members embraced each other at hello and goodbye.

☐ Fans and celebrities (total strangers) hugged each other for pictures and shared sharpies for autographs.

☐ The general public sat next to each other in movie theaters, crowded buses, trains, and airplanes.

☐ Concertgoers huddled together to get a closer look and a better picture of their favorite musical artist, while people were passed through the crowd to the stage by strange sweaty arms and hands.

The Coronavirus so rudely interrupted our natural human acts of love, care, and concern. Turning our displays of affection into isolation, suspicion, avoidance, fist bumps, and waves. It wasn't until we had to separate ourselves involuntarily from others that we realized how up close and personal we lived daily in the presence of our family, friends, co-workers, and community.

People really seemed mindful and respectful of the practice of social distancing for their safety and for others who they were in the company of. We became conscious of not invading another's space nor allowing someone to wander aimlessly into ours. When someone crowded our space, a simple step back reminded them that they were "too close for comfort."

Staying away from anything that you don't want to catch, receive, or give to others is a responsible way to handle a communicable disease like the Coronavirus or any other. Long before COVID-19 came along to this generation, Tuberculosis (TB) was dangerously feared, and similar social distance practices are still in place because of it. There are even vaccinations for TB to prevent spreading. It could be said that tuberculosis was the Coronavirus of its day. Serving as another example of an infectious disease before the COVID-19 occurrence. This is for everyone who felt like "poor us."

The extreme emphasis placed on social distancing and isolation was to prevent and slow down the spread of the Coronavirus disease in all sectors of society, homes, schools, stores, doctor's offices, hospitals, public events, and churches. We are grateful to our media outlets, healthcare facilities, and medical professionals for ensuring that we have been given the necessary information, which gives us safety advantages. However, there is another catastrophic disease that is lurking in the hearts, minds, and bodies of people that is spreading at an alarming rate.

It is spreading among youth, young adults, middle-aged, and seniors.

It has crossed oceans to other countries affecting all races of people. Faster than ministers, psychologists, psychiatrists, or prison inmates can warn the public. It is taking over, ruining lives, and causing premature death. It's sometimes subtle and often overt. This disease attacks and ravages the human soul. Its far-reaching effects have already caused havoc in the lives of many with devastating, life-altering results. A small word with such a large influence on mankind. SIN.

Health organizations scrambled to control and minimize the Coronavirus that rebelled and refused to be controlled, but slightly yielded to be managed at best. Just as medical scientists researched methods to slow the effects of the Coronavirus, clergy look for methods to slow the spread of SIN. A little 3 letter word with formidable, destructive power to destroy families, communities, neighborhoods, cities, states, countries, and nations.

Good Social Manners

Turning our heads and sneezing into the fold of our arms, coughing into our hands, discarding tissues in a trash can, and washing hands frequently are societal norms that should always be practiced whether there is a pandemic or not. No law should have to mandate good manners. Parents, guardians, and educators are responsible for teaching, training, and enforcing good old-fashioned, respectable manners. For people who were already conscious of the proper way to conduct themselves in the presence of others, the safety measures were only elevated habits because they were already routinely practicing them. For those who, as we say, didn't have or adhere to "home training," social distancing and combined safety actions became an annoyance because it was good manners times ten; for those who had not mastered good social manners beforehand.

Social and physical distancing may be a modern practice to shield against communicable sickness and disease, but it didn't start recently with the COVID-19 Pandemic. This discipline reaches all the way back to biblical records. We will now view this ancient practice from many centuries ago, but it is still being used today.

Biblical Social Distancing

But the practice of "maintaining a greater than usual physical distance" goes back to the 14th century, when ships arriving in Venice during an outbreak of the Black Death were forced to quarantine or sit at anchor for 40 days. The measure aimed to protect the city from the bubonic plague, which killed an estimated 25 million people in Europe.

It may have been the earliest public health measure ever recorded, said David Jones, M.D. '01, Ph.D. '01. But

there may have been even earlier measures, as suggested by biblical accounts of communities expelling people with Leprosy from their towns and villages.

Nowhere will you find a chapter in the Bible with the sub-title Social Distancing, but social distancing was essentially practiced just as we do today, in ancient times for various reasons. Ill folks were separated due to normal or abnormal body functions, sickness, disease, idolatry, and sinfulness.

Laws focused on health and welfare were put into place to protect the natural and spiritual lives of all citizens and particularly those who served God, to keep oneself away from the contaminants of ill health, sin, and eternal damnation. The Pentateuch (1st 5 books of the Bible) contained many laws for spiritual ceremonies, rituals, and society, including the separation and isolation of people with medical conditions.

We shall now discover scriptures from the Bible introducing social distancing for medical reasons. Leviticus is the book of the Bible that is commonly referenced for its laws and regulations. This Bible book covered God's spoken laws for offerings, consecration of priests, priestly ministry, forbidden foods, moral laws, ceremonial laws, and sexual immorality, just to name a few. Leviticus also covered medical conditions, including the following:

☐ Women *are socially distanced* after childbirth (Leviticus chapters 12:1-8).

☐ Lepers are *socially distanced* when diagnosed with Leprosy (Leviticus chapters 13-14).

☐ Men and Women are socially *distanced* due to bodily discharges (Leviticus 15).

☐ People *Social distanced* if they made is contact with the dead (Numbers 5:2**)**.

These are just some of the reasons people socially distanced, as recorded in the Bible. Many suffered from diseases then that were debilitating, crippling, and deadly because of the ancient health care system. We are now blessed with fancy, plush hospitals, in and outpatient clinics, effective medications, medical machines, specialty surgeons, doctors and nurses, and other various medical specialists, and medical scientists. The advancement of health care is directly related to the ability to save lives. Just as the Coronavirus was a disease to be respected and feared, so was Leprosy in ancient biblical accounts. Perhaps we can rid ourselves of the "woe is me" syndrome when we look at what other societies endured with less medical intervention. No matter what angle you focus on, we are blessed to be living in both a time of continuous healing miracles from God and medical advancement from man. We need both.

Leprosy was a medical condition that required social distancing and isolation.

This chronic disease must be a significant illness due to its many biblical references. The term "leprosy" (including leper, lepers, Leprosy, leprous) occurs 68 times in the Bible.

☐ 55 times in the Old Testament (Hebrew = *tsara'ath*)

☐ 13 times in the New Testament (Greek = *lepros, lepra*)

To grasp the severity of the effects of Leprosy in biblical writings, reading the biblical societal laws concerning this disease will allow you to understand why it was necessary for the strict governing of those who carried the disease. Pause now and perform the following directions:

✓ Stop reading now; place your bookmarker here on this page!

✓ Turn in your Bible to the Old Testament.

✓ Find and read Leviticus Chapter 13.

✓ Find and read Leviticus Chapter 14.

✓ Now, continue reading the remainder of this chapter.

What is Leprosy? (Aka Hansen's Disease)

And the LORD spoke to Moses and Aaron, saying: [2] "When a man has on the skin of his body a

swelling, a scab, or a bright spot, and it becomes on the skin of his body like body like a leprous sore, then he shall be brought to Aaron the priest or to one of his sons the priests. [3] The priest shall examine the sore on the skin of the body; and if the hair on the sore has turned white, and the sore appears *to be* deeper than the skin of his body, it *is* a leprous sore. Then the priest shall examine him and pronounce him unclean. Leviticus 13:1-3

Leprosy, also known as Hansen's disease (HD), is a long-term infection by the bacteria Mycobacterium leprae or Mycobacterium lepromatosis. Infection can lead to damage to the nerves, respiratory tract, skin, and eyes.

This nerve damage may result in a lack of ability to feel pain, which can lead to the loss of parts of a person's extremities from repeated injuries or infection through unnoticed wounds. An infected person may also experience muscle weakness and poor eyesight. Leprosy symptoms may begin within one year, but for some people, symptoms may take 20 years or more to occur. Wikipedia

While its definition in modern times is different from biblical times, there is no doubt that the definitions overlap, and the modern form of the disease still illustrates important spiritual lessons today.

Leprosy has terrified humanity since ancient times and was reported as early as 600 BC in India, China, and Egypt. Hansen's disease is still a major health problem.

The disease is a constant reminder of just how much things have changed since God pronounced a curse on the earth. At first, everything was "very good." https://answersingenesis.org/biology/disease/biblical-leprosy-shedding-light-on-the-disease-that-shuns/

How Does Leprosy Spread?

Leprosy is spread by multiple skin contacts and droplets from the upper respiratory tracts, such as nasal secretions transmitted from person to person.

Spread is thought to occur through a cough or contact with fluid from the nose of a person infected by Leprosy. Genetic factors and immune function affect how easily a person catches the disease. Leprosy does not spread during pregnancy to the unborn child or through sexual contact. Wikipedia

Leprosy and COVID-19 spread very similarly. Just as Leprosy has become a "hot topic" in the Bible amongst other illnesses, more than likely, so will COVID-19 in history books. One day students may have to do reports in school about the great Coronavirus Pandemic. Perhaps your children, grandchildren or great grandchildren will interview you one day as to what it was like to live through a historical time, and you can show them the pictures of you with your mask on, which is sure to spark some laughs.

I recall when I moved to Oklahoma that my father The Late Charlie Ellis Roberson Sr. asked me, did I know the history of Tulsa, Oklahoma about Black Wall Street, the Black Wall Street massacre, or about the Black Cowboys. I wasn't aware of any of it; therefore, he took the time to give me the history. Fascinating. I was then able to share it with my children. Coincidently, my son Kevaris was born in Lawton, Oklahoma. Both of my children attended school there, which is 3 hours from Tulsa Oklahoma.

Now we have lived through something that future generations will only read about in a history book.

Leprosy Symptoms

Its symptoms start in the skin and peripheral nervous system (outside the brain and spinal cord), then spread to other parts, such as the hands, feet, face, and earlobes. Patients with Leprosy experience disfigurement of the skin and bones, twisting of the limbs, and curling of the fingers to form the characteristic claw hand. Facial changes include thickening of the outer ear and collapsing of the nose.

Tumor-like growths called lepromas may form on the skin and in the respiratory tract, and the optic nerve may deteriorate. The largest number of deformities develop from loss of pain sensation due to extensive nerve damage. For instance, inattentive patients can pick up a cup of boiling water without flinching.

It was the work of Dr. Paul Brand (the late world-renowned orthopedic surgeon and leprosy physician) with leprosy patients that illustrated, in part, the value of sensing pain in this world. The leprosy bacillus destroys nerve endings that carry pain signals; therefore, patients with advanced Leprosy experience a total loss of physical pain. When these people cannot sense touch or pain, they tend to injure themselves or be unaware of injury caused by an outside agent. In fact, some leprosy patients have had their fingers eaten by rats in their sleep because they were totally unaware of it happening; the lack of pain receptors could not warn them of the danger.

According to Dr. Brand, the best example in the Bible of a person with Hansen's disease is the man with the withered hand (Mark 3:5; Matthew 12:13, Luke 6:10). He likely suffered from tuberculoid Leprosy; Biblical Leprosy.

In addition to pain and disfiguration, biblical Leprosy and Hansen's disease are both dreaded, and people were shunned (separated, socially distanced, isolated) because of them.

Common symptoms present in the different types of Leprosy include a runny nose; dry scalp; eye problems; skin lesions; muscle weakness; reddish skin; smooth, shiny, diffuse thickening of facial skin, ear, and hand; loss of sensation in fingers and toes; thickening of peripheral nerves; a flat nose from destruction of nasal cartilages; and changes in phonation and other aspects of speech production. In addition, atrophy of the testes and impotence may occur.

Leprosy can affect people in different ways. The average incubation period is five years. People may begin to notice symptoms within the first year or up to 20 years after infection. The first noticeable sign of Leprosy is often the development of pale or pink-colored patches of skin that may be insensitive to temperature or pain. Patches of discolored skin are sometimes accompanied or preceded by nerve problems, including numbness or tenderness in the hands or feet. Secondary Infections (additional bacterial or viral infections) can result in tissue loss, causing fingers and toes to become shortened and deformed as cartilage is absorbed into the body. A person's immune response differs depending on the form of Leprosy.

Approximately 30% of people affected with leprosy experience nerve damage. The nerve damage sustained is reversible when treated early but becomes permanent when appropriate treatment is delayed by several months. Damage to nerves may cause loss of muscle function, leading to paralysis. It may also lead to sensation abnormalities or numbness, which may lead to additional infections, ulcerations, and joint deformities.
Wikipedia

Spiritual Perception of Leprosy

For many centuries, Leprosy was considered a curse of God, often associated with sin. It did not kill, but neither did it seem to end. Instead, it lingered for years,

causing the tissues to degenerate and deform the body.
https://answersingenesis.org/biology/disease/biblical-
leprosy-shedding-light-on-the-disease-that-shuns/

When mankind faces disasters, the question of God's involvement always comes up. Even if it is not spoken, it is surely thought. Is God doing this to us or just allowing it to happen? Is it our own fault that we are in many of the messes that we find ourselves in? Is the Devil involved lurking nearby, laughing at our calamities?

The age-old question has been, "Why do bad things happen to good people?" However, I don't recall the question floating around, "Why do bad things happen to bad people?" Most of our mentalities are the same as guilty criminals who throw rocks and hide their hands. When murderers, thieves, and sexual predators are caught, arrested, and sentenced, they want to know why they received such harsh punishments like 30 years without parole, life in prison, or the death penalty. Uh, Da? Without Christ, we are bad and are deserving of anything that He does or allows. With Christ, we are "righteous" only because of Him. If you see any good thing in me, give God the praise and the glory. In the words of the gospel singing duo Mary Mary, "It's the God in me."

Perception of Leprosy in the Old Testament

Biblical Leprosy is a broader term than the Leprosy (Hansen's disease) that we know today. The Hebrew

tsara'ath included a variety of ailments and is most frequently seen in Leviticus, where it referred primarily to uncleanness or imperfections according to biblical standards. A person with any scaly skin blemish was *tsara'ath*. The symbolism extended to rot or blemish on leather, the walls of a house, and woven cloth. Other Old Testament references to Leprosy are associated with punishment or the consequences of Sin.

In the Old Testament, the instances of Leprosy most likely meant a variety of infectious skin diseases and even mold and mildew on clothing and walls.

https://answersingenesis.org/biology/disease/biblical -leprosy-shedding-light-on-the-disease-that-shuns/

Perception of Leprosy in the New Testament

In the Septuagint, the Greek translation of the Hebrew Bible, *tsara'ath* was translated as *the leprous*. These words in Greek implied a skin condition that spread over the body. Others have suggested that the translation of *tsara'ath* (to the leprous) includes "molds." The recent discovery of a highly toxic mold (*Stachybotrys sp.*), which contaminates buildings and causes respiratory distress, memory loss, and rash, lends support to the translation of *tsara'ath* to include "mold."

References to Leprosy have a different emphasis in the New Testament, stress God's desire to heal. Jesus freely touched people with Leprosy. While people with

Leprosy traditionally suffered banishment from family and neighbors, Jesus broke from the tradition. He treated lepers with compassion, touching and healing them.

In the New Testament it is also noted, *tsara'ath* incorporates a collection of contemporary terms, including Hansen's disease, infectious skin diseases, and mold (or even mildew) diseases.
https://answersingenesis.org/biology/disease/biblical-leprosy-shedding-light-on-the-disease-that-shuns/

.

Social Distancing of Lepers in the Bible

Leprosy was a disease that was not only communicable but gruesome, loathing, and disgusting to look upon and smell for both the leper and everyone. Ugly and Stink. Social distancing was probably a natural progression for lepers to remove themselves from people, and for people to distanced themselves from lepers, in addition to being declared unclean by the priest and mandated to isolate or join a colony of lepers.

But if the bright spot *is* white on the skin of his body and does not appear *to be* deeper than the skin, and its hair has not turned white, then the priest shall isolate *the one who has* the sore seven days. [5] And the priest shall examine him on the seventh day; and indeed, *if* the sore appears to be as it was, *and* the sore has not spread on the skin, then the priest shall isolate him another seven days. Leviticus 13:4-6

And he shall examine the plague; and indeed *if* the plague *is* on the walls of the house with ingrained streaks, greenish or reddish, which appear to be deep in the wall, then the priest shall go out of the house, to the door of the house, and shut up the house seven days. Leviticus 14:38

Whom the sore *is*, his clothes shall be torn and his head bare; and he shall cover his mustache, and cry, 'Unclean! Unclean!' He shall be unclean. All the days he has the sore, he shall be unclean. He *is* unclean, and he shall dwell alone; his dwelling *shall be* outside the camp. Leviticus 13:45

When the LORD said to Moses, "If her father had but spit in her face, would she not be ashamed seven days? Let her be shut out of the camp seven days, and afterward, she may be received *again.*" So Miriam was shut out of the camp for seven days, and the people did not journey till Miriam was brought in *again.* And afterward, the people moved from Hazeroth and camped in the Wilderness of Paran. Numbers 12:14-16

Although the terms are different in describing the state of the diseased patients of Leprosy and COVID-19. Each illness had its own descriptor to distinguish the sick person's status, whether ill or healed.

☐ Lepers were considered **UNCLEAN.**

But when raw flesh appears on him, he shall be unclean. And the priest shall examine the raw flesh and pronounce him to be unclean; *for* **the raw flesh** *is* **unclean. It** *is* **leprosy.** Leviticus 13:14-15

Coronavirus patients were considered **POSITIVE.**

COVID-19 Positive (SARS-CoV-2 RNA Detected) Test Result. If your COVID-19 test was positive, this means that the test did detect the presence of COVID-19 in your nasal secretions. This result would suggest that you are currently infected with COVID-19.

☐ Healed Lepers were considered **CLEAN.**

"And if leprosy breaks out all over the skin, and the leprosy covers all the skin of *the one who has* **the sore, from his head to his foot, wherever the priest looks, then the priest shall consider; and indeed** *if* **the leprosy has covered all his body, he shall pronounce** *him* **clean** *who has* **the sore. It has all turned white. He** *is* **clean. Or if the raw flesh changes and turns white again, he shall come to the priest. And the priest shall examine him; and indeed** *if* **the sore has turned white, then the priest shall pronounce** *him* **clean** *who has* **the sore. He** *is* **clean.** Leviticus 13:12-17

☐ Healed Coronavirus patients were considered **NEGATIVE.**

COVID-19 Negative (SARS-CoV-2 RNA Not Detected) Test Result

If your COVID-19 test was negative, this means that the test did not detect the presence of COVID-19 in your nasal secretions. This result would suggest that you are not currently infected with COVID-19.

Old Testament Lepers

King Uzziah (2 Chronicle 26:23)

He was the king of Judah who continued to lead while being ill. **So Uzziah rested with his fathers, and they buried him with his fathers in the field of burial which *belonged* to the kings, for they said, "He is a leper." Then Jotham, his son, reigned in his place.**

Captain Naaman (2 Kings 5:1-3 & 27)

He was a well-respected military soldier who carried out his duties with a health crisis. **Now Naaman, commander of the army of the king of Syria, was a great and honorable man in the eyes of his master because, by him, the LORD had given victory to Syria. He was also a mighty man of valor *but* a leper. And the Syrians had gone out on raids and had brought back captive a young girl from the land of Israel. She waited on Naaman's** wife. Then she said to her mistress, "If only my master *were* with the Prophet who *is* in Samaria! For he would heal him of his Leprosy." Therefore, the Leprosy of Naaman shall cling to you and your descendants forever." And he went out from his presence leprous, *as white* as snow.

Servant Gehazi (2 Kings 5:25-27)

He was a servant of the Prophet Elijah who set out to deceive to receive gifts in Elijah's name without his permission, which brought leprosy upon him. **Now he went in and stood before his master. Elisha said to him, "Where *did you go,* Gehazi?" And he said, "Your servant did not go anywhere." Then he said to him, "Did not my heart go *with you* when the man turned back from his chariot to meet you? *Is it* time to receive money and to receive clothing, olive groves and vineyards, sheep and oxen, male and female servants? Therefore, the Leprosy of Naaman shall cling to you and your descendants forever." And he went out from his presence leprous, *as white* as snow.**

Prophetess Miriam (Numbers 12:9-16)

Her and her brother Priest Aaron talked behind Prophet Moses' back because of something displeasing to them about Moses' wife and his close relationship with God. Therefore, God let them know just how he felt about it by striking her with leprosy. **So, the anger of the LORD was aroused against them, and He departed. And when the cloud departed from above the** tabernacle, suddenly Miriam *became* leprous, as *white as* snow. Then Aaron turned toward Miriam, and there she was, a leper. So, Aaron said to Moses, "Oh, my Lord! Please do not lay [*this* Sin on us, in which we have done foolishly and in which we have sinned. Please do not let her be as one dead, whose flesh is half consumed when he comes out of his mother's womb!" So, Moses cried out to the LORD, saying, "Please heal her, O God, I pray!"

Then the LORD said to Moses, "If her father had but spit in her face, would she not be ashamed seven days? Let her be shut[out of the camp seven days, and afterward, she may be received *again*." So Miriam was shut out of the camp for seven days, and the people did not journey till Miriam was brought in *again*. And afterward, the people moved from Hazeroth and camped in the Wilderness of Paran.

It is believed that Priest Aaron was not punished because Prophetess Miriam was the instigator.

Four Leprous Men at the Gate (2 Kings 7:3)

These gentlemen were socially distanced due to having Leprosy. They sat outside of the gate to beg for food and necessary daily supplies because they had to stay in the colony and couldn't go into the city gates until healed. **Now there were four leprous men at the entrance of the gate, and they said to one another, "Why are we sitting here until we die?**

New Testament Lepers

A Colony of Lepers (St. Luke 17:11-19)

Ten lepers who were desperate to be healed were bold enough to reach out to Jesus and cry with loud voices, depending on his mercy to heal them, and it worked. He did.

Now it happened as He went to Jerusalem that He passed through the midst of Samaria and Galilee. Then as He entered a certain village, there met Him ten men who were lepers, who stood afar off. And they lifted up *their* voices and said, "Jesus, Master, have mercy on us!" So when He saw *them,* He said to them, "Go, show yourselves to the priests." And so it was that as they went, they were cleansed. And one of them, when he saw that he was healed, returned, and with a loud voice glorified God, and fell down on *his* face at His feet, giving Him thanks. And he was a Samaritan. So Jesus answered and said, "Were there not ten cleansed? But where *are* the nine? Were there not any found who returned to give glory to God except this foreigner?" And He said to him, "Arise, go your way. Your faith has made you well."

One Leper (Matthew 8:1-4)

There was a leper who so boldly challenged the Lord to heal him. The leper showed faith that if Jesus wanted to. He could. And good thing that he asked because Jesus, without hesitation, healed him. We have not because we ask not. **When He had come down from the mountain, great multitudes followed Him. And behold, a leper came and worshiped Him, saying, "Lord, if You are willing, You can make me clean." Then Jesus put out His hand and touched him, saying, "I am willing; to be cleansed." Immediately his Leprosy was cleansed. And Jesus said to him, "See that you tell no one; but go your way, show yourself to the priest, and offer the gift that Moses commanded, as a testimony to them."**

This compilation of lepers includes both the elite and the common. It is an example of the indiscriminate Coronavirus. King Uzziah, Captain Naaman, Gehazi the servant, and Prophetess Miriam. They were all revered leaders, and they were leprous. The unnamed lepers and common citizens were affected by Leprosy too. We may accuse COVID-19 of many things, but being a respecter of people isn't one of them.

People indeed and unfortunately died from COVID-19. Since you are reading this book, that means that you survived. Therefore rejoice & do this:

✓ Put a book marker here for just a moment,

✓ Put the book down for a moment,

✓ Stop reading for a moment, and

✓ Take a moment to shout HALLELUJAH! I SURVIVED!

Thanks be to God, let's continue.

Stay 6 Feet Away From SIN

A sick body is a burden to carry daily, and deteriorating health demands much time, energy, and attention. But a sick mind, body, soul, and spirit demands immediate undivided attention.

We received instructions from the CDC and local authorities to stay 6 feet away from friends, family, co-workers, and strangers in proximity, to safeguard our health and theirs because safety is both offensive and defensive. We have a dual responsibility to protect ourselves and to protect others. So, it is as it pertains to Sin. If we are sin-sick, we should be accountable for separating and isolating ourselves in the presence of God until we have been healed and declared whole. And others have the same responsibility not to spread their spiritual illnesses to us. Thoughts, mindsets, ungodly habits, and addictions can all be caught and spread.

The Word of God admonishes us with this passage. **Therefore, come out from among them and be separate, says the Lord. Do not touch what is unclean, and I will receive you." "I will be a Father to you, and you shall be my sons and daughters, says the LORD Almighty."** 2 Corinthians 6:17-18

In other words, do not touch SIN. It can contaminate you. Run, jump, and hide. Social, physical distance and isolate yourself from these and any sins:

Sexual Immorality

In 1 Corinthians Chapter 5, unfortunately, and ashamedly there was a SIN-sick disease spreading, much worse than any physical disease; sexual immorality, and incest. The Apostle Paul demanded that the congregation mourn instead of being puffed up. He gave clear, emphatic instructions for the church to put the person away. Social distance and isolation from the spiritually infected germ carrier.

It is actually reported *that there is* sexual immorality among you, and such sexual immorality as is not even named among the Gentiles, *that a man has his father's wife!* [2] And you are puffed up, and have not rather mourned, that he who has done this deed might be taken away from among you. [3] For I indeed, as absent in body but present in spirit, have already judged (as though I were present) him who has so done this deed. [4] In the name of our Lord Jesus Christ, when you are gathered together, along with my spirit, with the power of our Lord Jesus Christ, [5] deliver such a one to Satan for the destruction of the flesh, that his spirit may be saved in the day of the Lord Jesus.

[6] Your glorying *is* not good. Do you not know that a little leaven leavens the whole lump? [7] Therefore purge out the old leaven, that you may be a new lump, since you truly are unleavened. For indeed Christ, our Passover, was sacrificed for us. [8] Therefore let us keep the feast, not with old leaven, nor with the leaven of malice and

wickedness, but with the unleavened *bread* of sincerity and truth.

I wrote to you in my epistle not to keep company with sexually immoral people. [10] Yet I certainly *did* not *mean* with the sexually immoral people of this world, or with the covetous, or extortioners, or idolaters, since then you would need to go out of the world. [11] But now I have written to you not to keep company with anyone named a brother, who is sexually immoral, or covetous, or an idolater, or a reviler, or a drunkard, or an extortioner—not even to eat with such a person.

[12] For what *have* I *to do* with judging those also who are outside? Do you not judge those who are inside? [13] But those who are outside God judges. Therefore "put away from yourselves the evil person."

Argumentative and Divisive People

In the book of Titus, Apostle Paul was writing to the ministry in Crete to correct their destructive behavior one to another. This church was embroiled in unproductive discussions, and Apostle Paul wrote and letter in order to put an end to it. **Avoid foolish disputes, genealogies, contentions, and strivings about the law; for they are unprofitable and useless. Reject a divisive man after the first and second admonition, knowing that such a person is warped and sinning, being self-condemned.** Titus 3:9-10.

Fornication, Uncleanness and Covetousness

Ephesians 5:1-16 sounds the alarm to watch for, recognize and avoid many natural and spiritual dangers. This lists filthiness, idolatry, and whoremongering, amongst many other deplorable SINS. [1]**Be ye, therefore, followers of God, as dear children;**[2]**And walk in love, as Christ also hath loved us, and hath given himself for us an offering and a sacrifice to God for a sweet-smelling savor.**[3]**But fornication, and all uncleanness, or covetousness, let it not be once named among you, as becometh saints;**[4]**Neither filthiness, nor foolish talking, nor jesting, which are not convenient: but rather giving of thanks.**[5]**For this ye know, that no whoremonger, nor unclean person, nor covetous man, who is an idolater, hath any inheritance in the Kingdom of Christ and of God.**[6]**Let no man deceive you with vain words: for because of these things cometh the wrath of God upon the children of disobedience.**[7]**Be not ye, therefore, partakers with them.**[8]**For ye were sometimes darkness, but now are ye light in the Lord: walk as children of light:**[9]**(For the fruit of the Spirit is in all goodness and righteousness and truth;)**[10]**Proving what is acceptable unto the Lord.**[11]**And have no fellowship with the unfruitful works of darkness, but rather reprove them.**[12]**For it is a shame even to speak of those things which are done of them in secret.**[13]**But all things that are reproved are made manifest by the light: for whatsoever doth make manifest is light**[14]**Wherefore he saith, Awake thou that sleepest, and arise from the dead, and Christ shall give thee light.**[15]**See then that ye walk** circumspectly, not as fools, but as wise,[16] Redeeming the time, because the days are evil.

Fleshly Deeds

When we make provision for the flesh, we make it convenient to SIN. Plotting and planning to do wrong on purpose is outright rebellion against God.

Now the deeds of the flesh are evident, which are: immorality, impurity, sensuality, idolatry, sorcery, enmities, strife, jealousy, outbursts of anger, disputes, dissensions, factions, envying, drunkenness, carousing, and things like these, of which I forewarn you, just as I have forewarned you, that those who practice such things will not inherit the Kingdom of God. Galatians 5:19-21

Abominations

It behooves us to remove ourselves from anything that God hates. He made it plain in the scriptures so that we can never say, "Oh, I didn't know that would be upsetting to God." **These six *things* the LORD hates, Yes, seven, *are* an abomination to Him: A proud look, A lying tongue, Hands that shed innocent blood, A heart that devises wicked plans. Feet that are swift in running to evil, A false witness *who* speaks lies, And one who sows discord among brethren.** Proverbs 6:16-19

These scripture passages are not directly related to the Coronavirus as far as your health is concerned, although ungodly practices can affect your health. But these verses are definitely related to your spiritual health. You can "catch" and be infected by someone else's SIN. Bad attitudes, negative mindsets, doubt, unbelief, ungodly habits, and immoral behavior can be spread when in proximity to spouses, children, family, friends, co-workers, influence from strangers (public opinion) and media, to cause you to become ill. Put space between you and anything or anybody that makes your mind, body, soul, or spirit sick.

Remember, during the pandemic, self-awareness was an independent skill that was expected of all citizens? In other words, "check yourself." Remember how conscious we were if we coughed, had a fever, were lethargic, or lost our appetite or sense of smell? We purposely paid attention and stayed aware of anything that seemed threatening to our health. Don't wait for the prophet or pastor to point out your shortcomings. When you fellowship with the Holy Spirit, both the good and the bad will be revealed. You will enjoy the presence of God without prohibition if you get it right and spend more time worshipping instead of repenting. Adopt this saying for a spiritual self-health check-up. "I better check myself before I wreck myself."

Your spiritual health is just as important as your natural health. Just as you make doctor's appointments when something uncomfortable and unusual is happening in your body, make an appointment with Dr. Jesus. Tell Him all about your suffering, and He will make you whole. Be cognizant of these sinful symptoms:

☐ If you are starting to doubt the Word of God, *social distance* from doubters.

☐ If you are starting to have a bad attitude, *social distance* from people who have not renewed their minds.

☐ If you are starting to pick up bad habits, like lying, gossiping, and using filthy language, then *socially distance* yourself from people with untamed, filthy tongues.

☐ If you are starting to skip church, *socially distance* yourself from people who fail to assemble themselves together.

If you are suffering from any of these spiritual health declines, social distance and isolate yourself in your prayer closet until you are made (again) into His image. Once you have obtained optimum health, guard it. The enemy of our soul is hiding in the shadows cooking up the next pot of SIN, sickness, and infirmity to put on you. Keep your distance from spiritually sick people who may reinfect you once you experience total healing.

Why Is Leprosy Also Called Hansen's Disease?

Leprosy was renamed Hansen's disease after Norwegian scientist Gerhard Henrik Armauer Hansen, who, in 1873, discovered the slow-growing bacterium now known as *Mycobacterium leprae* as the cause of the illness. In 1931, A patient named 'Stanley Stein printed the first issue of the 'Sixty-Six Star,' an in-house patient news sheet that later became "The STAR," with the mission to "Spread the Light of Truth on Hansen's Disease." The STAR(magazine) advocated changing the name of the disease called Leprosy to Hansen's disease to mitigate stigma and honor the Norwegian doctor who discovered Mycobacterium Leprae under the microscope in 1873. search.yahoo.com

Renaming SIN

Leprosy surely has made a bad name for itself. So, to remove the shock factor, it was renamed to remove the fright. Well, at least that was the intention. Pick the disease title that soothes your flesh, but both have potential to maim you.

Lessening the shock of devilish activities is a permeating process designed to gain acceptance so that it can be said: "It isn't so bad." People groups, politicians, educators, and the like who refuse to serve God change names and meanings to smooth over their SIN sickness.

☐ Adultery is now called entanglement.

☐ Lunatics are now labeled as mental health patients.

☐ Homosexuality is renamed named gay/same-gender loving.

☐ Sexual perversion is referred to as an alternative lifestyle.

☐ Immoral behavior is now known as challenges.

☐ Premeditated bad habits are called struggles.

☐ Abortion is now politically women's right to their bodies.

☐ Assisted suicide's new medical term is mercy killings.

If you change the name of a cow to duck. The cow will not start quacking, grow wings, and start floating on water. He will remain a cow no matter how many times you say, "Here ducky, ducky."

As we often say, "It is what it is." SIN is what it is.

And while I am writing, some people groups are whitewashing more terms to cover up sinful behavior with smooth words. Check the dictionary. One thing that has not changed is that God hates SIN, and it stinks in His nostrils. However, He sent His only begotten Son because He hates SIN, but God loves the sinner.

Imagine that your children go out to play and get dirty on purpose, by rolling in the mud, like a human pig. Then come into the house smelly, stinky, grimy, in modern terms, "funky." You don't want to throw them away like discarded trash. I'd hope you would not throw him or her in the dumpster to be picked up on trash day. First of all, if you are of African American descent, the first thing is that you will be told loud enough so that your neighbors will know that you stink (at least in my parent's house).

This will most likely be followed up by ensuring that their disdained garments are taken off, and they head to the nearest bathroom and take a bath or shower or both depending on how dirty he or she may be.

You will wash the dirty clothes or throw them away and buy new ones. Next comes a clean set of clothes, underwear, socks, and shoes will be waiting for him or her to finish up their bath. Now they are fresh and clean. You can now receive them with hugs and kisses and sniffs. And when they get dirty again, the cycle starts all over again. By now they should be conditioned to realize that being dirty is not pleasing to their parents and not healthy for them. This train of thought should minimize the number of times they purposely get dirty. Your sons and daughters are always assured that if they get dirty, they can always go home and get cleaned up. You will discard the dirt and keep the children.

So, it is with God. He wants to clean you up and provide you with new godly garments and keep you close to Him and away from the filthiness that He cleaned you up from. And that you grow to maturity and keep yourself clean. When it comes to your mind to lie, steal, or cheat, do you think of how disappointed that God will be, like the child that must face their parents for another hot shower or steam bath and maybe even a belt?

Therefore, having these promises, beloved, let us *cleanse* ourselves from all *filthiness* of the flesh and spirit, perfecting holiness in the fear of God.

For godly sorrow produces *repentance* leading to salvation, not to be regretted; but the sorrow of the world produces death. II Corinthians 7:1 & 10

If you are reading this, I know that the conviction of the Holy Spirit is overtaking you right now. This is not just a book you are reading; this is a Holy Spirit filled book written with the power to change lives. Yours. Today is the right day to change your life. Don't read this book in vain. Let me take that step alongside you.

✓ Put a book marker here on this page. Place the book down.

✓ Ask God to forgive you for not serving Him before by refusing salvation.

✓ Let Him know you are ready, right here and now.

✓ Begin to ask God to forgive you for all of your sins; call them out by name (known and unknown).

✓ Denounce Satan and his Kingdom. Take back your authority from him over your life.

✓ Accept a covenant with God to walk upright before Him.

✓ Receive it in your heart, and believe your life is changing right now.

Welcome to the family of God, my new brother and sister in Christ.

As soon as you can:

✓ Get water baptized by full immersion.

✓ Ask the Holy Spirit to dwell within you.

✓ Study God's Word (the Bible) day and night.

✓ Practice living according to the Bible without compromise.

✓ Develop godly relationships with other believers for accountability.

✓ Find a church home with Godly leaders with a good teaching ministry to get you grounded in your new-found relationship.

✓ Pray about your calling into ministry work.

✓ Get busy working in the Kingdom saving the spiritual lepers.

Now that you are on your way to a new way of living remember to:

SOCIAL DISTANCE, STAY 6 FEET AWAY FROM SIN!

Chapter 5: Personal Protection Equipment

O Lord, I have come to you for protection; don't let me be disgraced. Save me and rescue me, for you do what is right. Turn your ear to listen to me and set me free. Psalm 71:1-2

To receive expert advice, we must consult the experts. There is a lot to consume as it pertains to PPE Equipment. It is more than putting on gloves and placing a helmet on your head. There are various industries, different kinds of equipment, maintenance procedures and proper use. The one place that always provides accurate and up to date information on work related safety matters is OSHA. This organization exists for the sole purpose of developing, regulating, promoting, and enforcing safety protocols in the workplace for safety of workers. Let us familiarize ourselves with their mission.

What is the Occupational Safety and Health Administration (OSHA)?

The Occupational Safety and Health Administration (OSHA) is a federal agency in the United States committed to safeguarding worker health and safety.

Congress established OSHA in 1971, following its enactment of the Occupational Safety and Health Act of 1970. This groundbreaking legislation came in response to the growing concerns over workplace accidents that resulted in an alarming 14,000 worker deaths and 2.5

million disabled workers annually in the two years previous to the bill's passing.

Since its inception, OSHA has been a key player in transforming the landscape of worker safety across the nation. The agency's firm enforcement of workplace laws and standards, coupled with its commitment to providing training, outreach, education and assistance, have significantly contributed to making workplaces safer.

OSHA has been successful in slashing the work fatality rate by more than half and has achieved considerable reductions in overall injury and illness rates in industries where it has focused its attention, such as textiles and excavation. techtarget.com

What Is Personal Protective Equipment?

Personal protective equipment, commonly referred to as "PPE", is equipment worn to minimize exposure to hazards that cause serious workplace injuries and illnesses. These injuries and illnesses may result from contact with chemical, radiological, physical, electrical, mechanical, or other workplace hazards. Personal protective equipment may include items such as gloves, safety glasses and shoes, earplugs or muffs, hard hats, respirators, or coveralls, vests, and full body suits. osha.gov

Proper Use of Personal Protective Equipment?

Having PPE is the beginning step of providing protection from harm in dangerous situations. However, using it properly guarantees the optimum protection which that piece of equipment can provide. Your PPE must fit properly to protect properly.

All personal protective equipment should be safely designed and constructed and should be maintained in a clean and reliable fashion. It should fit comfortably, encouraging worker use. If the personal protective equipment does not fit properly, it can make the difference between being safely covered or dangerously exposed. When engineering, work practice, and administrative controls are not feasible or do not provide sufficient protection, employers must provide personal protective equipment to their workers and ensure its proper use. Employers are also required to train each worker required to use personal protective equipment. cdc.gov

Workers should be trained to know the following

☐ When is it necessary to wear PPE?

☐ What kind of PPE is needed in each situation?

☐ How to properly put on, adjust, wear and take it off PPE.

☐ The limitations of the PPE equipment to protect.

☐ Proper care, maintenance, expected life, and disposal of PPE.

PPE for Different Industries

Each industry has its own necessary type of personal protection equipment to protect the body from head to toe, to include, law enforcement, military personnel, manufactory workers, construction workers and medical health care workers.

☐ Face (masks or coverings), eye protection (goggles, eye shields, earplugs).

☐ Head (helmets, hats, head-coverings).

☐ Hand (heat and cold resistant gloves, emollients).

☐ Foot (boots, steel toe boots, compression sox)

☐ Body (vests, coveralls, bullet proof vests, knee pads, gowns, uniforms, duty belt suspenders) and shields.

COVID-19 PPE for the Public

During the COVID-19 Pandemic, PPE equipment extended from professionals in their respective work fields to everybody else to include you and me. We all had to "gear up" to face the unrelentless Coronavirus. Our supply included face masks or coverings, gloves, hand wash, hand sanitizer and disposable paper towels.

Keeping ourselves protected from disease takes awareness, discipline, and consistency. Even with all the protective measures some people still contracted COVID-19, but it lessens the chances of spreading or contracting the disease.

A healthy body is of the utmost importance for our natural health. But we cannot neglect to protect our spiritual health, that is often attacked by spiritual warfare. Before there was a CDC, there was God who had already prepared our spiritual Personal Protection Equipment before we even where aware that we needed to use it. Just as construction workers are protected from their head with a hard hat all the way down to their feet with steel toe boots, so are the soldiers that are enlisted in the Army of the Lord. The list of items that are named for our protection is the whole armour (armor) of God found in Ephesians 6.

Christian's Personal Protection Equipment

God gave all of His army of soldiers' personal protection equipment that we need to live a life of victory, the Whole Armour of God.

Just like the coronavirus ravished the bodies of those who were affected by the disease. There is an unseen enemy that desires to ravish our minds, souls, bodies, and spirits. Known by many names, Lucifer the fallen angel, the devil, the enemy, the evil one, also known as Satan. No matter what you call him. He hates us and we hate him. And if it wasn't for a loving God, Lucifer would have destroyed us all. His well thought out plan didn't work in heaven or in the garden with Adam and Eve, it won't work now for those who have been redeemed by Christ.

God foreknowing that we would be tempted, tested, and tried, by The Evil One, gave us everything that we need to always be prepared for the spiritual battles. We are in warfare for our generation, families, friends, employment, world events including global situations of sickness and diseases like the Coronavirus.

The Bible often illustrates the Christian life as a battle against sin and Satan. We are soldiers of Christ in a spiritual warfare (2 Corinthians 10:3, 4; 2 Timothy 2:3, 4). As Scripture says, "We do not wrestle against flesh and blood, but against . . . spiritual hosts of wickedness" (Ephesians 6:12). That's why the apostle Paul encourages Christians to "put on the whole armor of God, that you may be able to stand against the wiles of the devil" (vs 11)

Let's take a look at each piece of this spiritual armor and see how it can enable us to be victorious as soldiers for Christ in our battle against the "spiritual hosts of wickedness." bibleinfo.com .

Finally, my brethren, be strong in the Lord and in the power of His might. Put on the whole armor of God, that you may be able to stand against the wiles of the devil. For we do not wrestle against flesh and blood, but

against principalities, against powers, against the rulers of the darkness of this age, against spiritual *hosts* of wickedness in the heavenly *places*. Therefore, take up the whole armor of God, that you may be able to withstand in the evil day, and having done all, to stand.

Stand therefore, having *girded your waist with truth,* having put on the breastplate of righteousness, and having shod your feet with the preparation of the gospel of peace; above all, taking the shield of faith with which, you will be able to quench all the fiery darts of the wicked one. And take the helmet of salvation, and the sword of the Spirit, which is the word of God, praying always with all prayer and supplication in the Spirit, being watchful to this end with all perseverance and supplication for all the saints. Ephesians 6:10-18

Just as we took time to ensure that we were ready to face the outside world during the COVID-19 Pandemic with masks, gloves, hand sanitizer, disinfectant wipes, and immune support tablets, we must be prepared to face the enemy of our souls. It was thoroughly explained to us why each piece of PPE was important and how it is beneficial to keeping us safe. The equipment that God gave us will also keep us safe from the Devil's harm. We shall now make a correlation between the PPE that we use to protect ourselves from infectious diseases like the Coronavirus and the PPE that keeps us out of harm's way of the spiritual diseases that are present to attack our spiritual selves.

COVID-19 PPE Purpose & Use

Masks

Since the coronavirus can spread through droplets and particles released into the air by speaking, singing, coughing or sneezing, masks are very helpful to prevent the virus from spreading in crowded indoor public places, especially those that contain a mixture of vaccinated and unvaccinated individuals.

Protective masks characteristics

☐ **Made from several layers of tightly woven fabric and fits well over your nose and mouth to be an effective filter.**

☐ **Clean your hands with soap or hand sanitizer before putting the mask on or taking it off.**

☐ **Wear consistently and appropriately, not pulled down to breathe or talk, or worn under the nose.**

☐ **The mask conforms to your face without gaps so the air you breathe in and out flows through the mask rather than around the mask through gaps at the sides, top or bottom.**

☐ **Flexible nose bridge to conform to the face and prevent fogging of eyeglasses.**

☐ **Stays in place while talking and moving requiring you to touch less.** hopkinsmedicine.org

Gloves

Wearing gloves can create a false sense of safety because people may not wash their hands as often if they have worn gloves. In that case contamination can be spread. Protect hands from contaminations, if touching or cleaning possible contaminated surfaces or caring for a COVID-19 patient.

The use of medical gloves is recommended as part of standard precautions to reduce the risk of contamination of healthcare workers' hands with blood and other body fluids including contact with non-intact skin and mucous membranes. When indicated, use of medical gloves is recommended as part of contact precautions, to reduce the risk of pathogen dissemination to the patient's environment, to other patients and for the protection of healthcare workers. https://www.ecdc.europa.eu

Proper donning & removal of gloves

☐ Remove accessories, rings, bracelets, watches etc.

☐ Wash your hands thoroughly with soap and water.

☐ Dry hands with a disposable towel.

☐ Place on gloves.

☐ Remove gloves by pulling if one finger at a time

☐ Dispose of in the trashcan

123

Hand Sanitizer

Hand Sanitizer does not replace soap and water. It should be used along with soap and water or when soap and water is unavailable. Soap and water remove debris from your hands. Hand sanitizer is most effective with clean hands.

The active ingredient in hand sanitizer is ethyl alcohol or isopropyl (rubbing) alcohol. These ingredients kill bacteria and viruses, including the coronavirus by dissolving their protein layer.

But the ingredient alone isn't enough: It also needs to be the right strength. Check the label to see if it contains at least 60% ethyl alcohol or 70% isopropyl alcohol.

"The alcohol content must be high to kill the coronavirus or any other germs," says Dr. McWilliams. "That's why I don't recommend people try to make their own sanitizer. If the alcohol isn't the right strength, the product won't disinfect." Health.clevelandlinic.org

Be sure to cover all surfaces of the hand and wrist.

Disinfectants (wipes or liquids)

Keeping surfaces that you use disinfected gives you the assurance of a safe place to work and play.

You can reduce the risk of potential spread of the virus that causes COVID-19 by regularly cleaning frequently touched surfaces. These may include tables, doorknobs, light switches, handles, counters, desks, toilets, faucets and sinks. Clean after you've had visitors. And clean more frequently if someone in your household is at increased risk of severe illness from COVID-19.

Clean with a product that is suitable for each surface. Follow the instructions on the product label.

Cleaning with soap and water removes dirt and lowers the number of germs on surfaces. Disinfecting can help kill any remaining germs.

When using a disinfectant, read the product label and follow instructions carefully, including what precautions to take when using the product. Many disinfectants need to stay on surfaces for some time to be effective. This is called the contact time.

Start by putting on gloves before disinfecting preferably disposable gloves, throw them away immediately after you're done. If you only have reusable gloves, don't use them for any other purposes. Wash your hands thoroughly with soap and water for 20 seconds immediately after cleaning and disinfecting.

Keep doors or windows open and use a fan to help increase ventilation while disinfecting your home. https://www.mayoclinic.org

Full Armour of God: PPE Purpose and Use

The spiritual armor that God has provided for us serves a purpose in spiritual warfare. He gave it to us to protect ourselves and to make advances to the Enemy's camp. It is up to us to be ready to employ our weapons at any time. We are fully covered.

We do not wrestle against flesh and blood. The Bible often illustrates the Christian life as a battle against sin and Satan. We are soldiers of Christ in a spiritual warfare (2 Corinthians 10:3, 4; 2 Timothy 2:3, 4). As Scripture says, "We do not wrestle against flesh and blood, but against . . . spiritual hosts of wickedness" (Ephesians 6:12). That's why the apostle Paul encourages Christians to "put on the whole armor of God, that you may be able to stand against the wiles of the devil" (verse 11).

Let's take a look at each piece of this spiritual armor and see how it can enable us to be victorious as soldiers for Christ in our battle against the "spiritual hosts of wickedness." Bibleinfo.com

#1 Belt of Truth

A soldier is only ready for battle when he is girded with his belt. A Roman soldier's belt was made of metal and thick heavy leather and was the carrying place for his sword. It also had a protective piece that hung down in the front. His belt held all other pieces of his armor together. To be fitted with his belt, meant he was ready to face action.

Truth is the belt that holds the believers' armor together as well. Ultimate Truth can be found in God's Word and in the person of Jesus Christ (John 14:6). We must know this Truth to protect ourselves against our flesh, the world, and the Father of Lies. Truth grounds us and reminds us of our identity in Christ. connectusfund.org

Behold, You desire truth in the inward parts, And in the hidden part You will make me to know wisdom. Psalm 51:6

#2 Breastplate of Righteousness

The Roman soldier was always equipped with a breastplate. This piece of armor protected his vital organs in the heat of the battle when he wasn't quick enough to take up his shield. The breastplate was for the quick and unexpected advances of the enemy.

As believers, we have no righteousness apart from that which has been given us by Christ. Our breastplate is His righteousness. His righteousness will never fail.

Though we have no righteousness of our own, we must still, by His power, chose to do right. Living a right life, rooted in God's Word is powerful in protecting our heart, killing our flesh, and defeating the enemy. connectusfund.org

He who follows righteousness and mercy, finds life, righteousness, and honor. Proverbs 21:21

#3 Sandals with the Gospel of Peace

Roman soldier's feet were fitted with sandals called caligae. These sandals were made to help protect soldier's feet during their long marches into battle. They had extremely thick soles and wrapped perfectly around their ankles in a way that protected against blistering. Caligae also had spikes on the bottom to help them stand firm as they traveled. This helped them have a firm foundation.

Believers also have a firm foundation in the Gospel. As believers, we have peace in knowing we are secure in what Jesus has done for us. connectusfund.org

And how shall they preach unless they are sent? As it is written: "How beautiful are the feet of those who preach the gospel of peace, who bring glad tidings of good things!" Romans 10:15

#4 Shield of Faith

The Roman soldier's shield was a complex piece of armor. The shield, also called a scutum, was a soldier's primary defensive weapon. It was made of impenetrable wood, leather, canvas, and metal and could be doused in water to extinguish the fiery arrows of the enemy. connectusfund.org

So, Jesus said to them, I say to you, if you have faith as a mustard seed, you will say to this mountain, 'Move from here to there,' and it will move; and nothing will be impossible for you. Matthew 17:20

#5 Helmet of Salvation

The Soldier's head is one of his most vulnerable areas. Without his helmet, one blow to the head would prove fatal. His helmet covered his entire head, facial area, and between the eyes. His armor would prove useless if he wasn't equipped with his helmet. connectusfund.org

But You, O LORD, are a shield or me, my glory and the One who lifts up my head. Psalm 3:3

#6 Sword of the Spirit

All other pieces of the soldier's arsenal are defensive weapons, but not his sword. The sword, a gladius, was a deadly weapon. In the hands of a skilled warrior, he could pierce through even the strongest armor.

Our sword is the Word of God, both the written and the incarnate Word. Every other piece of armor protects us against attacks. With God's Word, we are truly able to fight and defeat all enemies. Christ used Scripture to defeat Satan when He was tempted in the desert. We must do the same. connectusfund.org

For the word of God is living and powerful, and sharper than any two-edged sword, piercing even to the division of soul and spirit, and of joints and marrow, and is a discerner of the thoughts and intents of the heart. Ephesians 4:12

#7 Prayer

In prayer, we show our reliance upon God to act and move. Our entire armor is rooted in His strength. Without His presence, we are powerless in the fight. We must fight on our knees. The One who has won the war is with us in the battle. We will see a victory when we fight in His power. connectusfund.org

[6] Be anxious for nothing, but in everything by prayer and supplication, with thanksgiving, let your requests be made known to God; [7] and the peace of God, which surpasses all understanding, will guard your hearts and minds through Christ Jesus. Philippians 4:6-8

When you are fighting the wiles of the enemy like sickness and disease in the body, remember that your armor serves offensively for protection and defensively for the ability to assault.

"Behold, I have created the blacksmith, who blows the coals in the fire, who brings forth an instrument for his work; And I have created the spoiler to destroy. No weapon formed against you shall prosper, and every tongue which rises against you in judgment, you shall condemn. This is the heritage of the servants of the LORD, and their righteousness is from Me" says the LORD. Isaiah 54:16-17

God forms special instruments for our battles with the Full Armour of God,

Personal Protection Equipment!

Chapter 6: COVID-19 Vaccines and Boosters

Or do you not know that your body is the temple of the Holy Spirit *who is* in you, whom you have from God, and you are not your own? For you were bought at a price; therefore glorify God in your body and in your spirit, which are God's. 1 Corinthians 6:19-20

Much controversy stirred over getting vaccinated or not for the Coronavirus. Some were all for the vaccinations and boosters, hook, line, and sinker. Some were all against the vaccinations and boosters with conspiracy theories to back them up. Some had trust in the medical system and applauded the medical scientist, while yet others were distrusting and suspicious of this sudden "quick fix."

The topic of the "shot" was trending in personal conversations, social media platforms, and news outlets. People even begin to put up banners around their social media pictures with "I am vaccinated." "Stay home, save lives," was the new trend. While others warned the public not to get the shot, claiming that worse health problems would occur or maybe even death. There were "no holds barred" on either side. Just when I thought that all of the excitement was in the professional boxing ring, professional boxers could take a few pointers on how to effectively hit below the belt.

There was great division. But what we all agreed on was that we wanted to find a way to make COVID-19 go away as fast as possible, by any means necessary. The Health Professionals presented a COVID-19 vaccines and boosters as part of the answer.

Results of COVID-19 Vaccines and Boosters

☐ People received the vaccinations and boosters and lived.

☐ People received the vaccinations and boosters and died.

☐ People received the vaccinations and boosters and stayed in their current health state.

☐ People received the vaccinations and boosters, and their health declined.

☐ People received the vaccinations and boosters and became well, never to be infected again.

☐ People received the vaccinations and boosters and became infected again, some more than once.

There were varying opinions between the sick and afflicted, healthy and whole, medical institutions and families of the sick patients.

I remember, as a little tyke getting ready for "big school," that I and my siblings, at the age-appropriate time, had to get shots in order to go to school. And looking back now, it was very strictly monitored and documented with the form from the doctor. And if any children slipped in with a promise from their parents, they had to be picked up from school until there was proof that the child had been vaccinated.

As an adult now experiencing the COVID-19 Pandemic I finally understand what all of the hoopla was all about.

How Do Vaccines Work?

Vaccines work by teaching your immune system to recognize certain viruses. After you receive a vaccine, your body will be more prepared to fight back. Vaccines help prevent or reduce the severity of the illness if you are exposed to the virus that causes the disease. Wedovaccines.com

Facts About the COVID-19 Vaccine

☐ COVID-19 vaccines help our bodies develop immunity to the virus that causes COVID-19 without us having to get the illness.

☐ Different COVID-19 vaccines may work in our bodies differently, but all provide protection against the virus that causes COVID-19.

☐ None of the COVID-19 vaccines can *actually* give you COVID-19.

☐ Different types of vaccines work in different ways to offer protection. But with all types of vaccines, the body is left with a supply of "memory" T-lymphocytes as well as B-lymphocytes that will remember how to fight that virus in the future.

☐ It typically takes a few weeks after vaccination for the body to produce T-lymphocytes and B-lymphocytes. Therefore, it is possible that a person could be infected with the virus that causes COVID-19 just before or just after vaccination and then get sick because the vaccine did not have enough time to provide protection.

☐ Sometimes, after vaccination, the process of building immunity can cause symptoms such as fever. These symptoms are normal signs the body is building immunity.

☐ Vaccines do not use any live virus.

☐ Vaccines cannot cause infection with the virus that causes COVID-19 or other viruses.

☐ Vaccines do not affect or interact with our DNA. These vaccines do not enter the nucleus of the cell where our DNA (genetic material) is located, so they cannot change or influence our genes. cdc.gov

Different Types of COVID-19 Vaccines

During the Coronavirus Pandemic, there were choices as to which kind of vaccine you could receive. It may have depended on your health provider, when the vaccine was released in your area and availability. You could, in essence, "shop around" for a vaccine.

Normally it is nice to have choices if you are choosing from a restaurant menu or from a shelf full of designer purses or new tools for house renovations. But choosing a vaccine with all the hard-to-pronounce medical terms, ingredients, side effects, pre-existing health conditions, quality of the research, and various manufacturers seemed like too many choices for lay people. The answer we were looking for is, "Which one works the fastest and is the safest?" Give us that one!

Here is simplified information in layman's terms to help us to understand the functions of the various vaccines from wedovaccines.com.

All COVID-19 vaccines prompt our bodies to recognize and help protect us from the virus that causes COVID-19.

There were three types of COVID-19 vaccines for use in the United States: MRNA, protein subunit, and viral vector vaccines.

MRNA

Messenger RNA vaccines, or mRNA vaccines, are a newer type of vaccine. This vaccine teaches our cells to

make a protein that mimics the one on the surface of the virus. Once our body creates this protein, the immune system learns to recognize it as a target and gets ready to fight against the real virus when it comes along.

mRNA vaccine technology is currently being used to make some of the COVID-19 vaccines. They've also been studied against other diseases, such as Ebola and Zika.

While you may have heard that mRNA vaccines can alter a person's DNA, they are not able to do this.

Protein Subunit

Instead of using the whole virus, protein subunit vaccines use just a small piece of the virus. They teach your body how to recognize the actual virus and attack it when needed.

Scientists created the first protein subunit vaccine in the 1980s to help prevent Hepatitis B. For decades, this technology has been used for many other vaccines, including Shingles and Human Papillomavirus (HPV). Novavax is using the same well-established technology for our vaccine development today. Wedovaccines.com

Whole virus vaccines are made using a weakened or inactivated version of the virus it intends to fight. Since it uses an inactivated form of a virus, it cannot infect your cells and make you sick. However, it can still trigger an immune response. This response can help prevent illness if you come into contact with or are exposed to the live virus.

This type of technology has been used for rabies and Hepatitis A vaccines.

Viral Vector

Viral vector vaccines work by using a changed, harmless virus. This is called the "vector." A vector is like a vehicle that carries instructions to our cells on how to fight against a particular disease.

Hundreds of scientific studies have been done and published worldwide on viral vector vaccines, and they have been around for decades. Some vaccines recently used for Ebola outbreaks have used viral vector technology. Studies are still being done to see if they can be used to help prevent infectious diseases such as Zika, influenza, and HIV.

As of May 6, 2023, the J&J/Janssen COVID-19 vaccine, a viral vector vaccine, has expired and is no longer available for use in the United States. None of these vaccines can give you COVID-19.

The COVID-19 Vaccine Booster

A COVID-19 booster shot is an additional dose or dose of a vaccine given after the protection provided by the original shot(s) has begun to decrease over time. The booster helps people maintain strong protection from severe Coronavirus disease.

We can fight off sickness and disease when we are at our level of optimum health, with strong immune systems.

Vaccines and boosters help when the strength of our own natural immune systems needs a "boost" to help to keep our bodies healthy and strong. This should be a lifestyle for us to be as healthy as we can be daily. Why wait for a national health crisis to come along to be concerned about your body?

Every day that you wake up is a day to enjoy life and live it to the fullest. If you are riddled with sickness and disease, your quality of life will be minimum. There are family generational illnesses that are handed down to us unwillingly or unfortunate health situations that happen to us that are sometimes related to our local or work environment. Some jobs come with environmental dangers. Think about the firemen who run into burning buildings. Though they are equipped with the proper personal protection equipment, years of this type of work may cause deteriorating health eventually to lungs and limbs. But the stronger your body is, the more you preserve the natural fighting abilities that your body has.

There have been reports of whole communities that have taken ill due to pollution or buried chemicals underneath housing communities resulting in group lawsuits. These are what I like to call the "uncontrollable" factors. However, there are daily healthy habits that you can control to ensure you are fortifying your body with the proper nutrients needed to be healthy and whole that is within your power.

Many people already had compromised immune systems and pre-existing conditions, which made them more susceptible to the Coronavirus. It is of the utmost importance that we make our health a priority. What I believe the Coronavirus did was reveal where we were health-wise, individually and as a society.

When faced with the decision of whether to be vaccinated or not to be vaccinated, it came down to personal choice, your health, job requirements, and your doctor's recommendation.

Benefits of a Healthy Immune System

A well-working immune system prevents germs from entering your body and kills them or limits their harm if they get in. To keep your immune system healthy, make sure you adapt healthy lifestyle habits (see below) for a lifetime of optimum health. Make it a daily routine, not just a reaction to an emergency health crisis.

Healthy Lifestyle Habits for a Healthy Immune System

☐ Get plenty of sleep. The recommended amount from the sleep experts are 7 to 9 hours. Set a bed- time and stick to it.

☐ Stay active with exercise or fun activities that keep you moving. Take the stairs instead of an elevator. Take regular walks. Follow a safe exercise routine approved by your doctor.

☐ Eat healthy foods and include plenty of fruit, vegetables, and water. Limit fast foods and "junk" foods.

Cook healthy foods and order healthy foods when you eat out.

☐ Manage your weight by finding out from your doctor what your Body Mass Index is (BMI) and use that as a goal for optimum health. Extra weight places extra stress on the body and namely the heart.

☐ Reduce your stress. Find healthy way to cope with stressful situations. Read, exercise, watch a movie, or speak affirmations from the bible out loud.

☐ General healthful habits. Take medications according to directions. Eliminate alcohol, drugs and smoking of cigarettes, cigars etc. to keep rich oxygen in your blood stream, flowing throughout your body.

What Is Our Immune System Is Made Of?

When we think of important or major organs, our brain, kidney, heart, liver, spleen, or pancreas may come to mind. However, our immune system is comparably important because it regulates our body's ability to fight off illnesses.

Your immune system is a large network of organs, white blood cells, proteins (antibodies), and chemicals. This system works together to protect you from foreign invaders (bacteria, viruses, parasites, and fungi) that cause infection, illness, and disease.

A Properly Working Immune System

Knowing how your immune system works will give you an understanding of how to guard it and make sure that it stays strong and is working properly.

When your immune system is working properly, it can tell which cells are yours and which substances are foreign to your body. It activates, mobilizes, attacks, and kills foreign invader germs that can cause you harm. Your immune system learns about germs after you've been exposed to them too. Your body develops antibodies to protect you from those specific germs. An example of this concept occurs when you get a vaccine. Your immune system builds up antibodies to foreign cells in the vaccine and will quickly remember these foreign cells and destroy them if you are exposed to them in the future. Sometimes doctors can prescribe antibiotics to help your immune system if you get sick. But antibiotics only kill certain bacteria. They don't kill viruses.

When your immune system is not working properly it can't mount a winning attack against an invader, a problem, such as an infection, develops. Also, sometimes your immune system mounts an attack when there is no invader or doesn't stop an attack after the invader has been killed. These activities result in such problems as autoimmune diseases and allergic reactions. my.clevelandclinic.org

Help For Our Spiritual Immune System

Vaccinations work from the inside out, whereas gloves, hand sanitizer, soap, and water work only on the outside. God, in his infinite wisdom knew that once man had fallen that he would need something that worked on the inside, so that outside behavior would represent His character.

There are so many things that attack our spiritual immune system, attempting to wear us down and take over our minds, bodies, souls, and spirits to make us so weak, that we are not able to fight off spiritual diseases. If we can't fight off the devilish germs, bacteria, and viruses, we will find ourselves susceptible to all types of spiritual illnesses, just like what happens when our natural immune system is compromised. Our quality of health may become so poor, we may be left without the ability to ward off those unhealthy dangers which cause severe damage to our spiritual man.

We need the Holy Spirit to help us in our weaknesses, just as the vaccinations and boosters were designed to help to strengthen our immune systems. When was the last time you had a spiritual immune system check-up? If you can't remember when or it has been a long while, now is a good time.

Romans 8:26, **Likewise the Spirit also helps in our weaknesses. For we do not know what we should pray for as we ought, but the Spirit Himself makes intercession for us with groanings which cannot be uttered.**

Just as vaccinations had to be injected on the inside of the body to fight what is destroying the body from the inside, so must we have an internal deposit of something

143

potent and powerful to fight carnality from the inside out. Sin is in plenteous supply. Ungodly temptations are vying for my attention and yours. The antidote for the spiritual ills of the children of God is the Holy Spirit.

I am reminded of a song that says, "Something on the inside, working on the outside, bringing about a change in me." "The Holy Ghost on the inside, working on the outside, bringing about a change in me." Patients who were diagnosed with COVID-19 were full of hope that the shot would improve their health. It is an educated guess and a gamble. However, we are 100% sure that the Holy Spirit will improve our lives. It has been tried and proven by a long list of witnesses, including me.

Ephesians 5:18, **And do not be drunk with wine, in which is dissipation; but be filled with the Spirit.** Being filled is being occupied on the inside. We have access to the strongest force that has ever existed, which is the Holy Ghost, also known as the Holy Spirit. It is the power that created the worlds, distributed gifts, raised Jesus Christ from the dead and will quicken our mortal bodies from the grave unto eternity.

I cannot attest to the power of any vaccinations or boosters as it pertains to the body. Nor have I obtained a medical degree in medicine or medical research. But I can confidently testify to the power of the Holy Ghost and I can truly say, that I am not the same person I was before I yielded my life to Jesus Christ, because of an inward change.

The Apostle Paul testified of the power of the Holy Spirit, and how it worked in his life to keep him strong from a natural weakness in his body. He said it was a thorn in his flesh. **Three times I pleaded with the Lord to take it away from me. 9 But he said to me, "My grace is sufficient for you, for my power is made perfect in weakness." Therefore, I will boast all the more gladly about my weaknesses so that Christ's power may rest on me. 10 That is why, for Christ's sake, I delight in weaknesses, in insults, in hardships, in persecutions, in difficulties. For when I am weak, then I am strong.** 2 Corinthians 12:8-10.

Just as the Coronavirus patients understood that they needed something stronger than the virus to kill the virus, so do we know that we need something stronger than the flesh to kill the flesh.

Romans 8:1-28, **There is therefore now no condemnation to them which are in Christ Jesus, who walk not after the flesh, but after the Spirit.[2] For the law of the Spirit of life in Christ Jesus hath made me free from the law of sin and death.**

[3] For what the law could not do, in that it was weak through the flesh, God sending his own Son in the likeness of sinful flesh, and for sin, condemned sin in the flesh.[4] That the righteousness of the law might be fulfilled in us, who walk not after the flesh, but after the Spirit.[5] For they that are after the flesh do mind the things of the flesh; but they that are after the Spirit the things of the Spirit.[6] For to be carnally minded is death; but to be spiritually minded is life and peace.

[7] Because the carnal mind is enmity against God: for it is not subject to the law of God, neither indeed can be. [8] So then they that are in the flesh cannot please God.

[9] But ye are not in the flesh, but in the Spirit, if so be that the Spirit of God dwell in you. Now if any man have not the Spirit of Christ, he is none of his.

[10] And if Christ be in you, the body is dead because of sin; but the Spirit is life because of righteousness. [11] But if the Spirit of him that raised up Jesus from the dead dwell in you, he that raised up Christ from the dead shall also quicken your mortal bodies by his Spirit that dwelleth in you. [12] Therefore, brethren, we are debtors, not to the flesh, to live after the flesh. [13] For if ye live after the flesh, ye shall die: but if ye through the Spirit do mortify the deeds of the body, ye shall live. [14] For as many as are led by the Spirit of God, they are the sons of God.

[15] For ye have not received the spirit of bondage again to fear; but ye have received the Spirit of adoption, whereby we cry, Abba, Father. [16] The Spirit itself beareth witness with our spirit, that we are the children of God: [17] And if children, then heirs; heirs of God, and joint-heirs with Christ; if so be that we suffer with him, that we may be also glorified together. [18] For I reckon that the sufferings of this present time are not worthy to be compared with the glory which shall be revealed in us. [19] For the earnest expectation of the creature waiteth for the manifestation of the sons of God. [20] For the creature was made subject to vanity, not willingly, but by reason of him who hath subjected the same in hope,

²¹ Because the creature itself also shall be delivered from the bondage of corruption into the glorious liberty of the children of God.²² For we know that the whole creation groaneth and travaileth in pain together until now.

²³ And not only they, but ourselves also, which have the firstfruits of the Spirit, even we ourselves groan within ourselves, waiting for the adoption, to wit, the redemption of our body.²⁴ For we are saved by hope: but hope that is seen is not hope: for what a man seeth, why doth he yet hope for?²⁵ But if we hope for that we see not, then do we with patience wait for it.²⁶ Likewise the Spirit also helpeth our infirmities: for we know not what we should pray for as we ought: but the Spirit itself maketh intercession for us with groanings which cannot be uttered.

²⁷ And he that searcheth the hearts knoweth what is the mind of the Spirit, because he maketh intercession for the saints according to the will of God.

²⁸ And we know that all things work together for good to them that love God, to them who are the called according to his purpose.

The Holy Spirit serves a necessary function in our lives, to warn us and to ward off contaminants from us. You may see many "praise breaks" circulating on social media, and it is delightful to feel the Spirit of God. You may run, shout, dance, scream and speak in tongues, because the Spirit is a powerful force when we encounter it in and upon our flesh.

But the Holy Ghost serves a far greater purpose than to give you energy, goose bumps and another language. The Holy Ghost serves as your spiritual vaccination and booster. You may be running low on your initial infilling of the Spirit, because you have extended yourself with prayer and spiritual warfare. If so, get you another "boost" of the Holy Ghost. You can be filled over and over and over again. And the best part is that there is no waiting period in between and no long lines to stand in. I was filled with the Holy Ghost in a house holding hands in a circle with a group of Christian women while we were praying. It can happen instantaneously. It is yours for the asking. Anytime and anywhere, right now. Apostle Paul came upon a group of people who were believers in need of being filled, but were not aware that there was a Holy Spirit that was available to them.

And it happened, while Apollos was at Corinth, that Paul, having passed through the upper regions, came to Ephesus. And finding some disciples [2] he said to them, "Did you receive the Holy Spirit when you believed?"

So, they said to him, "We have not so much as heard whether there is a Holy Spirit."

[3] And he said to them, "Into what then were you baptized?"

So, they said, "Into John's baptism."

[4] Then Paul said, "John indeed baptized with a baptism of repentance, saying to the people that they

should believe on Him who would come after him, that is, on Christ Jesus."

⁵ When they heard *this,* they were baptized in the name of the Lord Jesus. ⁶ And when Paul had laid hands on them, the Holy Spirit came upon them, and they spoke with tongues and prophesied. ⁷ Now the men were about twelve in all. Acts 19:1-7

Just as simple as it happened for them and to them, it can happen to you, if it hasn't already. Are you ready? If so, do this now:

✓ Put a book marker on this page.

✓ Put the book down.

✓ Turn in your Bible to the New Testament,

✓ Read the full version of Act 16:25-34 **Then he (prison guard) called for a light, ran in, and fell down trembling before Paul and Silas. ³⁰ And he brought them out and said, "Sirs, what must I do to be saved?"³¹ So they said, "Believe on the Lord Jesus Christ, and you will be saved, you and your household." ³² Then they spoke the word of the Lord to him and to all who were in his house. ³³ And he took them the same hour of the night and washed *their* stripes. And immediately he and all his *family* were baptized. ³⁴ Now when he had brought them into his house, he set food before them; and he rejoiced, having believed in God with all his household.** Acts 16:29-34

✓ If you haven't accepted Christ as your Savior, ask out loud for your sins to be forgiven and accept his atonement for your sins, in your own words.

✓ Began to worship and praise God, you will feel a physical presence come over you and your voice begin to change to what may sound like an unrecognizable language. Do not resist it, yield. This is one of the signs of being Holy Spirit filled.

✓ Practice your language daily when you pray for yourself and others. Your language will mature from gibberish to a fluent language. It is the Holy Spirit praying for, through and with you.

✓ Ask the Holy Spirit to reveal to you by interpretation what you are praying for in your new language. Write it down and ask the Holy Spirit to bring it to pass.

✓ Read Romans Chapter 8 to get a foundation of this new phenomenon that has just taken place.

Just as the COVID-19 vaccines and boosters have side effects, I must warn you to watch out for the side effects of being filled with God's power of the Holy Spirit. You will experience power over the enemy, yoke destroying anointing and righteous living. HALLELUJAH! Congratulations for yielding yourself as a vessel of God.

Now follow the example that Apostle Paul and Apostle Silas set. Ask people everywhere you go. "Have you been filled with the Holy Spirit since you believed? If they are not a believer, lead them to Christ.

If they are, do as Paul did, lay hands on them to receive the Holy Spirit and instruct them to pray for others. Now that you have the power you can pray for another to receive it. Pray it forward. Let us get the whole world filled with the power of God.

The Holy Spirit's power exceeds the power of,

COVID-19 VACCINES AND BOOSTERS!

Chapter 7: I Have Escaped to Tell You

Behold, the LORD's hand is not shortened, that it cannot save; Nor His ear heavy, that it cannot hear. Isaiah 59:1

Job has received much recognition for what he faced when he was afflicted by Satan. But let us not be guilty of overlooking some "unsung heroes" in this story. They are not named, but their testimonies are attributed to the mercy of our God, who sits high and looks low. This chapter is sure to lift up hung-down heads and lift-up sorrowful Spirits.

13 There was a day when his sons and daughters were eating and drinking wine in their oldest brother's house; 14 and a messenger came to Job and said, "The oxen were plowing and the donkeys feeding beside them, 15 when the Sabeans raided them and took them away indeed they have killed the servants with the edge of the sword, and I ALONE HAVE ESCAPED TO TELL YOU!"

16 While he *was* still speaking, another also came and said, "The fire of God fell from heaven and burned up the sheep and the servants and consumed them, and I ALONE HAVE ESCAPED TO TELL YOU!"

17 While he *was* still speaking, another also came and said, "The Chaldeans formed three bands, raided the camels and took them away, yes, and killed the servants with the edge of the sword; and I ALONE HAVE ESCAPED TO TELL YOU!"

¹⁸ While he *was* still speaking, another also came and said, "Your sons and daughters were eating and drinking wine in their oldest brother's house, ¹⁹ and suddenly a great wind came from across the wilderness and struck the four corners of the house, and it fell on the young people, and they are dead, and I ALONE HAVE ESCAPED TO TELL YOU!"

²⁰ Then Job arose, tore his robe, and shaved his head; and he fell to the ground and worshiped. ²¹ And he said: "Naked I came from my mother's womb, and naked shall I return there. The LORD gave, and the LORD has taken away; Blessed be the name of the LORD."

²² In all this, Job did not sin nor charge God with wrong. Job1:13-22

When reading this story, I was sorrowful for Job and his wife and the surviving family members of the servants who died during these tragic events. I have always been intrigued by the messengers who escaped to tell Job the unfortunate news. Although they were the bearers of bad news, they lived to tell the story with a combination of gladness and grief. Glad to be alive to tell what happened, no matter how awful the report was. But also grieving the lost lives of so many. Especially to a man that was perfect and upright in eyes of God. We may have experienced these same exact emotions. Glad to be alive but sorrowful for the fallen soldiers of COVID-19.

It is perfectly clear that Job did absolutely nothing to deserve these devastating events.

There was a man in the land of Uz, whose name *was* Job, and that man was blameless and upright and one who feared God and shunned evil. Job1:1

Job did nothing wrong, but still lost everything except his life and his wife. Job's wife told him to curse God and die, but God let her live without any accidents or incidents. Interesting. The Lord and I will have to have a conversation about that when I get to Heaven. There isn't an indication that even those who lost their lives were guilty of God's wrath. The messengers of Job experienced the favor of God in this situation and were left to tell. As we reflect back over the Coronavirus ordeal, that was the prayer, that was the goal, to escape with our life.

Though there were millions of people who met their demise, many lived and are able to share their stories. We will now listen to several stories to see how they fought the battle of COVID-19 and won.

COVID-19 SURVIVORS

What I found interesting is that some of the people whom I am acquainted with who were infected with COVID-19, were the people who followed all the safety protocols consciously, intently, and rigorously. They were so strict with their regime that they could have been spokesmen and spokeswomen for the CDC. But they still were diagnosed with the Coronavirus, but survived its often, fatal blow.

Testimonies inspire, encourage, and ignite hope. That is exactly what we all need during these difficult times. Hope. Although the Coronavirus is no longer a public health crisis currently, people affected and their families are still coming to grips with the devastation in the aftermath. Here are stories of survivors that will surely lift up your spirit.

Pastor Chelec Pinckney

It was September 2020 when I caught "Covid." And I can't be mad or upset or even say "God, why me?" because the Bible says, "Time and chance happens to us all." Ecclesiastes 9:11. Which means we are all subject to go through something at any given time.

When I first caught Covid-19, I had no clue that I had the virus. I was still working out and walking and all the stuff that I normally do. I remember before the effects of Covid-19 really set in, I had a dream. In this dream, I was in the backyard of my dream home. The grass was beautiful and green, like I like it, and my daughter and I were sitting under an umbrella. Then all of a sudden, Michael Myers (the spirit of death) shows up with a big knife in his hand, and he looks at me, and he says, "Somebody has to die."

And I looked back at him and said, "Ain't nobody dying here." When I said that a black and white cat was walking all around the yard and he picked up the cat and stabbed it. Two days later I developed this cough. And every time I coughed, it felt like little sharp pieces of glass were sticking me all over my body. It caused me to get tested, and I tested positive for Covid-19.

At my worst, I felt like I was going to die. And I told God, I said, "If this is my time to go, you owe me nothing, and I'm grateful to you for allowing me to raise my five children to be adults." When my youngest daughter heard me say that, she began to pray. She laid hands on me and said, "God, you can be reasoned with," and when she said that, I said "God, all the teachings I taught these children over the years, they remembered." Just hearing her say that blessed my soul; I knew at that point, my labor was not in vain. Oh, and she prayed heaven down that day.

How God turned it around for me. My oldest daughter made me a concoction of garlic, bittersweet orange, lemon, apple cider vinegar, raw honey, and ginger. The next day I was a totally different person, glory be to God.

Audie Silcott Sr.

The word "Positive" gave me one of the most negative feelings I'd ever felt in my life. Positive for Covid-19 is what the results said. It was a stunning feeling, and I stared at the results for about five minutes. You see, I contracted COVID in mid-December of the first year it was labeled a pandemic. Every day, they had a number of COVID-19 related deaths continuously plastered on the news. Every day, every week, every month, it would reach a milestone. There was no vaccine available yet, and there was certainly no cure. Watching these numbers rise every day to unbelievable numbers was a very unsettling feeling. I just knew that if I contracted this awful disease, I would assuredly be one of those numbers going across the screen. But despite my best efforts to stay out of harm's way, I was diagnosed with Covid-19.

No one really knows how and when they contracted Covid-19, but I can say that I was on a film set from Friday to Sunday. I always kept my mask on, and even when it was time for lunch, I went outside and ate in my car. I always used hand sanitizer quite a bit. I really did try. However, by Monday evening, I felt chills all over my body. I decided to isolate myself and I took my temperature, which was normal. My breathing was fine, and I didn't have a cough, just the chills. By the next day, I had a headache and was feeling somewhat fatigued, which didn't go away. That's when I decided to get tested. My thoughts were with my children and the rest of my family upon receiving the news that I had contracted COVID-19. Of course, everyone was upset, as I was the first in my immediate family to get it. In my head, I was preparing to fight this thing and thought I was not going to let this get the better of me. At the same time, a little part of me was also preparing for the worst. And so, I waited, expecting the symptoms that I had heard so much about. It was as if I was in an army trench somewhere, waiting for the enemy to strike. I was on the lookout and dug in deep when the next shot was fired.

I was in the bathroom putting on deodorant when I noticed that I didn't notice a scent from it. I put it closer to my nose, and still nothing. I almost shoved the deodorant up my nostrils while taking deep breaths. Nothing! No smell? I hit the laundry room and opened a bottle of bleach, and took a whiff. Still nothing! As if that wasn't enough, I went to the kitchen and pulled a bottle of ammonia from under the sink. Nothing! By then, I started to feel a little lightheaded. It never occurred to me that just

159

because I didn't smell anything, doing what I did would not have an effect on me. I said to myself, "Let me stop before I end up passing out." My loss of taste diminished but never quite went away fully. I got a lot of advice on what to take for it. My family and friends were great. They brought me all kinds of vitamins, teas, mixes of turmeric, ginger, lime, orange juice, zinc; you name it. Those were my army buddies. They weren't going to leave me behind, even if they had to drop items off at my front door so I could retrieve them once they were a safe distance away.

I have to say, the one thing that made a noticeable difference was downing a pure ginger shot. Within 20 minutes, my fatigue was gone. I felt like I had all the energy in the world. I got up and cleaned my entire home. Every time I consumed the ginger, I felt noticeably better. Of course, I believe all the other items helped too. I even ordered a pulse oximeter to monitor my oxygen. It was as if ginger was my shield, and the other items were bullets. It was a war! I went on fighting day by day and documenting on my phone, what I was going through every day. As I said, just a little part of me was preparing for the worst. So, just in case, I at least wanted there to be a record. One thing I was gearing up for was the shortness of breath. That was the one part of the enemy that scared me the most.

Several times throughout the day, I would hold my breath for as long as I could to make sure I knew when the shortness of breath was coming. The longest I was able to hold my breath was up to 42 seconds. Well, the shortness of breath never came. I'm not quite sure how I would have handled that if it did. By the grace of God, I was spared that part. The fight went on, and eventually, the other symptoms went away. All but one remained. I still couldn't smell anything. No hint, sensation, or hue of a scent. Just cool air. It was the strangest thing. It was not until my birthday that I received the results that read "Negative." This, ironically, gave me one of the most positive feelings of joy. To know that I had beaten this awful disease that so many others did not.

Then realization and sadness set in, because it hits you just how blessed you were to have survived Covid-19 and feel saddened for those that did not. It was a bittersweet moment for me. There, I had survived Covid-19, and the only physical scar left was my loss of smell.

I went about my life, thinking that any day now, my smell would return. That went on for about three months, then, one day, a scent graced my nostrils. It was not a familiar scent, but a scent, nevertheless. I thought this was it; any day now, I would get my full smelling abilities, given to me at birth back. I was in for a rude awakening. This process would be slow as molasses going up a hill. Gradually, the sensation that I got back initially kept getting stronger, but it was just this one scent. It was not offensive, but I only had this one scent, no matter what I smelled. Everything smelled the same.

Eventually, I started to differentiate one smell from another. It was as if my brain had to learn, all over again, what was what when I smelled something. Once that started happening, one of my first thoughts was, "Wow, this world stinks!" Think about it, after not smelling anything at all for months, you get used to it. The house could have been burning down, and I would not have known it until it was probably too late! Anyhow, I had to learn to smell all over again, and to date, I would venture to say that I probably have about 70% of my smelling back. I'll take it, because leave it to Covid-19, I could have gone the rest of my life thinking that "my stuff don't stink." That wouldn't have been good at all.

Psychologically speaking, battling Covid-19 during the first year of the outbreak really messes with your mind. It gave me a new perspective on life. I still have work to do here while I still have air in my lungs.

Brina Mills

'Twas a day in January of 2022, when all through the house, there was a creature coughing; his name is My Spouse. He coughed, and he coughed, giving me such a scare, that COVID-19 could soon be here. There we both were, in our own little space, when hubby decided to cough in my face! I turned 'round quickly before the damage was done. But, two days later, I wasn't having fun!

COVID-19 had surely come; the fatigue, fever, and body aches were bothersome. I slept through the day and all through the night, no doctor visits or hospitals, only God's guiding light. The moment I took my eyes off the Prize, was the moment I had to desperately realize. That it's my faith and hope that's going to get me through, for God is My Healer and knows what to do. I was never vaccinated but thank God I've always been activated - by the Word of God. Therefore, being surrounded by His peace and presence did not make things hard. Though daily activities were affected quite a bit. I couldn't take two steps without wanting to sit.

I attended church services while online, but when I returned, things took some time. I couldn't praise and shout like I used to do, these post-COVID symptoms took some getting used to. Shortness of breath, tiredness, and fatigue are definitely things that I do not need! Routine phone calls and check-ins from family and friends, added to my care, days on end.

The greatest lesson I learned is, if you put all your trust in the Man with the Plan, the plans of man will not withstand.

May those lives lost, forever, be remembered.

April Johnson

My name is April Johnson. I experienced COVID-19, and it was the least of my worries at the time! I am unsure of how I contracted the virus. It was during the time I was fresh in mourning due to the sudden death of my father. Not only did I get ill with the virus right after his funeral, but so did my daughter. We both started feeling unwell; the first sign of the virus was a burning sensation in our noses. The feeling of needing to sneeze and discomfort lasted all day. The following day we were dealing with congestion in our head and nasal area. There was no fever, thankfully, so we did not feel really sick, but were dealing with cold-like symptoms. The way we found out it was COVID-19 was through a test at our doctor's office, because it was required for both me and my daughter to go back to work. We had to have a negative test. Once confirmed, we were both out of work for about a week, though the worst part of the illness had already passed, which was in the first three days. Overall, we were out of work and were in recovery for the better part of two weeks.

I would say the worst part of having COVID-19 for me was the fact that I could not breathe through my nose, and I would wake up in the middle of the night to sit up and catch my breath. I never developed any fever, cough, or chest congestion. Thankfully we made it through with no hospitalizations or emergencies. My daughter had to get tested several times until it showed negative results. I didn't take the test, but we had it at the same time, so I assumed I was ok (and I am). God is Good!

Ruth Johnson

My name is Ruth Johnson. I contracted COVID-19 right before the Omicron variant was announced. My husband and I isolated ourselves and discouraged our children or other guests from coming to visit. My symptoms were that of a mild flu. I did have a mild fever for a couple of days and was able to treat it with over-the-counter Ibuprofen. The way I found out that it was COVID-19 was convenient, as I was already scheduled for a routine checkup with my doctor. I explained the symptoms, and they tested me, and it was positive. By that time, there was nothing left for me to do but continue treating the symptoms as I had been. I drank my teas, consumed extra vitamins (including Vitamin C and B12), and drank plenty of fluids.

The worst moment of my bout with this virus was when I had what felt like maybe a panic attack, where I felt a little disoriented or unsettled. This was when I had been battling symptoms for maybe about 4 or 5 days. It was concerning to my husband, and he was ready to take me to the hospital, but I stayed home, continued with my medications, and prayed to God for my healing. I made it through that night and got better each day after that. I would say the illness lasted about two weeks or so. During that time, of course, I didn't leave the house except for the doctor's visit. Thankfully during this illness, I never developed a cough or breathing problems. I didn't confirm being negative after it was all over, but I just remained cautious and continued wearing my mask and social distancing as much as possible.

And even though neither I nor my husband had the vaccine administered, my husband never caught the virus himself. Glory to God for his mercy and grace!

Billy Mathis

It was the month of July, a Monday, the year 2020, in the a.m. I felt good that morning but not great. I had been feeling strange for about a week prior, which made me contact my doctor. After a phone evaluation, I was told that I don't have any of the known COVID-19 symptoms, but I should continue to take the necessary precautions. This Monday, I decided to take a jog, you know, in an attempt to feel normal.

The jog was 1-2 miles, and I did not feel any worse once I completed the run. I stopped several homes from mine, speaking with my childhood friend and neighbor Charlie Ellis Roberson II (the beloved deceased brother of the author). Once I departed, returning home was inviting, feeling ok after all. Entering my bedroom, I sat on the bed, and I felt the urge to spit. I went into the bathroom, and all I saw was blood in my mouth and coming out of my nose.

I lost it! Clearing my throat, nose, and mouth until it apparently was clear. I called for transportation to the hospital. All the while, on the ride to the medical facility was terrifying, since many people had lost their lives from COVID-19 at this point. Once again, I was cleared from not having COVID-19. I was treated for a bloody nose and released.

By Thursday, I was sick, and getting out of bed was very difficult. I was experiencing difficulty breathing. I was lethargic and very weak. I began consuming everything either hot or piping hot to the point it was as hot as I could take it. Every day I was asked for the next several weeks, to give samples, have a colonoscopy, along with a mental evaluation. They all came back negative, including the mental part, LOL.

In closing, I gradually gained weight but never reached 196; the closest I came was 185. I currently weigh about 180 lbs., and I'm told that I am pretty healthy in spite of my age. During this COVID-19 ordeal, I experienced: trauma, fear, and loneliness and was desperate to find answers to why my overall health was compromised. During this, I changed my diet even more so than I previously did, by removing pork, reducing my meat intake, and increasing my herbal tea intake along with mineral consciousness of foods. Thankful to have not succumbed to COVID-19. And not once did I ever test positive for it. But three people I was around all contracted it.

The Author: Ramona Roberson Gregory

I want to end with my own testimony concerning my experience with COVID-19. It is befitting to share my story of survival and triumph of how I overcame and lived to write this book.

First, unlike the previous storytellers, when I became ill, I was not aware of the Coronavirus, because it had not been announced or declared as a pandemic in the United States. My story begins in the latter part of November, and at the beginning of December 2019, I became functionally ill, meaning I continued with my normal daily activities. The date at the time was not significant; I had no idea I would be sharing my story in this book. To me, it was the wintertime when colds and flu were more common. I was annoyed and uncomfortable at worst.

I believed that I had caught a "bad cold" or a light case of the flu, with symptoms of light fever, chills, coughing, congestion of the nose and throat, shortness of breath, phlegm in my throat, and unable to lay down flat. I took strong cold medicine from over the counter about twice a day (for one who despises taking medicine) and drank plenty of water, clear fluids, and teas with honey, lemon, and lime often. However, it was an inconvenience; but I was not sidelined. I continued with my employment, personal, and ministry activities. What bothered me the most was that I did not understand why it lingered so long. I couldn't recall having cold symptoms for that extended period of time before. I never considered going to the doctor for a "common cold" or light flu, except this was not so common. "Oh well, I reasoned, some sicknesses had to run their course at their own time." And this was one of them.

After three weeks, close to a month, I was nearly back to 100 percent. As far as I was concerned, I had finally won the battle of a cold or flu that didn't want to let go of me, but I was the victor in shaking it off, with my health back to normal.

After COVID-19 was announced, it became obvious that the United States was in a public health crisis. As I listened to the symptoms on social media, in the news, and in conversations; these symptoms sounded all too familiar from over 4 to 5 months ago. It dawned on me one day that

I felt that way months ago, but there were no news reports at that time, nor did I visit a doctor for any diagnosis. I never go to the doctor if I believe the outcome is going to be a prescription that I already have in my medicine cabinet. Therefore, I was never inclined to make a doctor's appointment.

Around September 2021, from my recollection, I begin to feel fatigued. I am nocturnal and have cycles of sleep crashing involuntarily when I don't rest enough, so that's what I thought was happening again. I have been going to bed too late and getting up too early I thought. However, soon I began to feel the same symptoms again from 2019, already forementioned, but now I was well-aware of COVID-19.

Therefore, I took two days off work to rest and monitor my symptoms. I remember sleeping most of the first 48 hours only waking to eat and utilize the restroom. The extended weekend gave me enough time to start feeling like myself again, and it quickly passed completely about the time I returned to work. At this time, we had a strict policy at work for everyone to stay in their own offices, therefore I had little or no contact with my co-workers, which caused me to feel comfortable going back to work with home medication remedies with the mindset to keep to myself to keep others safe.

When I returned to work, my supervisor asked me, "Do you have COVID?" I said, no, I'm not claiming COVID-19 and I kept on working. I didn't have a test to verify or deny, but it sure was possible. By now, I was no longer suffering any remote symptoms anyway.

At this time, our workshops were being taught online or socially distanced in the classroom. The staff, including me, and the customers had to have on a mask the entire time in our facility. Therefore, I was safe from customers, and they were safe from me.

At this time, I was also attending worship services remotely, therefore, safe from congregants.

I shared with my music manager, Audie Silcott how I felt, and he asked, "Do you have COVID?" My answer was, "I don't know." We were told by news outlets what to do if we were sick during this time for any common reason, and the doctors expected "self-care." The hospitals at the time were a dangerous place to be with all the sick COVID-19 patients there. I live alone and felt quite comfortable in my own home with my own home remedies. My one stipulation during this time was, if I began to have trouble breathing, to the hospital, I would have gone. I was breathing normally, with no reason to "panic."

My thought process was that not every cough or sneeze is COVID-19, the common cold and flu are still prevalent. My body could be experiencing anything besides COVID-19. I was not going to jump on the bandwagon of fear. I have been my normal healthy self ever since; thanks be to God.

I never was diagnosed by a doctor nor spent any time in the emergency room or hospital. I am truly grateful that the Holy Spirit eradicated every germ, bacteria, and virus that was present in my body at that time.

I am delighted to report to you that all symptoms passed and never returned. I have not been sick since then, up until the very writing of this book. To God be the Glory!

The God of Restoration

Job lived through his trial, you lived through yours, these storytellers lived through theirs, and I lived through mine. Maybe you suffered loss during this treacherous time. Perhaps a vehicle, a job, your place of residence, your health, savings, or investments. Well, in case you haven't heard, God is a restorer, and He is known not just to add to your life but to multiply exponentially. So be encouraged and ask God for restoration. Not only is He able, but He desires to meet all our needs. Put Him to the test.

All ended well for Job, and since you are reading this book, it ended well for you too. Please accept my most sincere condolences if you lost a friend, co-worker, neighbor, or family member. Keep the great memories of the loved ones lost, love on the ones that are still present and the new lives coming into the world. May God restore unto you a heart of joy.

¹⁰ And the Lord restored Job's losses when he prayed for his friends. Indeed, the Lord gave Job twice as much as he had before. ¹¹ Then all his brothers, all his sisters, and all those who had been his acquaintances before came to him and ate food with him in his house; and they consoled him and comforted him for all the adversity that the LORD had brought upon him. Each one gave him a piece of silver and each a ring of gold.

¹² Now the Lord blessed the latter *days* of Job more than his beginning; for he had fourteen thousand sheep, six thousand camels, one thousand yokes of oxen, and one thousand female donkeys. ¹³ He also had seven sons and three daughters. ¹⁴ And he called the name of the first Jemimah, the name of the second Keziah, and the name of the third Keren-Happuch. ¹⁵ In all the land were found no women *so* beautiful as the daughters of Job, and their father gave them an inheritance among their brothers.

¹⁶ After this, Job lived one hundred and forty years and saw his children and grandchildren *for* four generations. ¹⁷ So Job died, old and full of days.

The messengers were surrounded by tragedy, but the tragedy passed them by. It is possible that they had bruises, battered bodies, and broken bones from the ordeals, but nevertheless they escaped as we did.

Since you are reading this book now, that means that you have escaped to tell. With gratitude, lastly do this:

✓ Put a book marker on this page.

✓ Put the book down.

✓ Say this after me in the words of Job," **"Naked I came from my mother's womb, and naked shall I return there. The Lord gave, and the Lord has taken away; Blessed be the name of the Lord." "Job did not sin with his tongue, and neither will I.**

✓ Repeat after me, "My life is more than material things. Anything that I have lost, God can restore. My turnaround serves as a testimony to the miraculous love, power, and restoration of God."

At the beginning of the Coronavirus Pandemic, I said to Mr. Audie Silcott (above story). "I will not die of the Coronavirus." He asked, "How do you know?" I replied "Because I have too much work left to do for God." Songs to write and sing, sermons to preach, and more. And here I am! The Coronavirus Pandemic is gone, but I am still here. I truly believe that God left me alive to write this book, to impart a spiritual perspective to the masses, to share these testimonies, and to encourage you.

Psalm 103:1-5

Bless the LORD, O my soul;
And all that is within me, *bless* His holy name!
² Bless the LORD, O my soul,
And forget not all His benefits:
³ Who forgives all your iniquities,
Who heals all your diseases,
⁴ Who redeems your life from destruction,
Who crowns you with lovingkindness and tender mercies,
⁵ Who satisfies your mouth with good *things,*
So that your youth is renewed like the eagle's.

I can say as Job's messengers said,

I HAVE ESCAPED TO TELL YOU!

SALUTATION

During the Coronavirus Pandemic in 2020, I started ministering Facebook live, in order to do my part as a minister to keep people encouraged during that difficult time. The Spirit of the Lord lead me to take the "terms" that we used often during this ordeal and teach using them as foundational lessons. I humbly obeyed and created a series entitled "Four Sermons in 4 Saturdays." I ministered on some of the topics from this book. You Are Essential Workers, First Responders, Let's Go, COVID-19 and Social Distance, Stay 6 Feet Away from Sin.

At that time, I was using it for encouragement by taking the plight that we were facing and giving it a Biblical perspective with courage, hope and victory. I was pleasantly surprised when God led me to write this book by building on those principles that I had previously taught.

As I wrote He had me to add the additional chapters to give a well-rounded reminder of all that we have overcome. Through it all, I am so glad I lived to write about it, and I am so glad that you lived to read about it.

May we all benefit from the lessons learned from the COVID-19 health crisis. And may we be prepared if faced with a similar ordeal. This book leaves us without excuse.

Your time is precious; therefore, I hope that you found these lessons to be a good use of your time.

Finally, when faced with life's challenges, remember **"Do Not Panic, this is just a test".**

--Ramona Roberson Gregory

Made in the USA
Columbia, SC
14 November 2023

26124505R00100